DATE DUE

NOV 1 3 2012	
NOV 2 7 2012	
JAN 2/2013	
JAN 2 4 2013	
FEB 0 2 2013	
FEB 0 2 2013	
MAR - 6 2013	
SEP 0 8 2016	

BRODART, CO.   Cat. No. 23-221

D1378436

CAKE POPS

LITTLE CAKES, BITE-SIZE COOKIES, SWEETS AND PARTY TREATS ON STICKS

CAKE POPS

70 irresistibly original miniature delights, shown in 200 step-by-step photographs

HANNAH MILES

With photography by Nicki Dowey

LORENZ BOOKS

This edition is published by Lorenz Books,
an imprint of Anness Publishing Ltd,
Blaby Road, Wigston, Leicestershire LE18 4SE
info@anness.com

www.lorenzbooks.com; www.annesspublishing.com

If you like the images in this book and would like to
investigate using them for publishing, promotions or
advertising, please visit our website www.practicalpictures.com
for more information.

w OCT 1 1 2012
$19.99

Publisher: Joanna Lorenz
Editor: Kate Eddison
Photographer: Nicki Dowey
Food stylist: Aya Nishimura
Prop stylist: Wei Tang
Designer: Lisa Tai
Production controller: Steve Lang

All rights reserved. No part of this publication may be
reproduced, stored in a retrieval system, or transmitted in any
way or by any means, electronic, mechanical, photocopying,
recording or otherwise, without the prior written permission of
the copyright holder.

PUBLISHER'S NOTE

Although the advice and information in this book are believed
to be accurate and true at the time of going to press, neither
the author nor the publisher can accept any legal responsibility
or liability for any errors or omissions that may have been
made nor for any inaccuracies nor for any loss, harm or injury
that comes about from following instructions or advice in this
book. All sticks and skewers used in these recipes must be
suitable for food use. For recipes where the sticks are baked,
the sticks must also be ovenproof. Pointed skewers are not
suitable for children.

© Anness Publishing Ltd 2012

NOTES

Bracketed terms are intended for American readers.

For all recipes, quantities are given in both metric and imperial
measures and, where appropriate, in standard cups and spoons.
Follow one set of measures, but not a mixture, because they are
not interchangeable.

Standard spoon and cup measures are level. 1 tsp = 5ml,
1 tbsp = 15ml, 1 cup = 250ml/8fl oz.

Australian standard tablespoons are 20ml. Australian readers
should use 3 tsp in place of 1 tbsp for measuring small quantities.

American pints are 16fl oz/2 cups. American readers should use
20fl oz/2.5 cups in place of 1 pint when measuring liquids.

Electric oven temperatures in this book are for conventional ovens.
When using a fan oven, the temperature will probably need to be
reduced by about 10–20°C/20–40°F. Since ovens vary, you should
check with your manufacturer's instruction book for guidance.

The nutritional analysis given for each recipe is calculated per
portion (i.e. serving or item), unless otherwise stated. If the recipe
gives a range, such as Serves 4–6, then the nutritional analysis will
be for the smaller portion size, i.e. 6 servings. The analysis does
not include optional ingredients, such as salt added to taste.

Large (US extra large) eggs are used unless otherwise stated.

AUTHOR'S ACKNOWLEDGEMENTS

With many thanks to Kate Eddison for her patient editing of this
book and to Joanna Lorenz for letting me indulge my cake pop
dreams. To Aya Nishimura for the beautiful food styling and
Nicki Dowey for the gorgeous photography – thank you for
making my recipes look so special. Particular thanks also to
Heather, Ellie and Claire of HHB agency for their continued
support, and to my family and friends who tasted all the pops in
this book – you are all stars! Finally, I would like to thank Gregg
Wallace, MasterChef judge extraordinaire (and lover of a good
buttery biscuit base), for his kind endorsement of this book.

Contents

Introduction

Welcome to the wonderful world of pops – cake pops, cookie pops and other yummy treats on sticks. From the classic truffle-style cake pops and buttery crumble cakes to crisp meringues and chewy cookie pops, there is a favourite in this book for everyone.

Although the trend for cake pops (chocolate candy-coated mini cakes on sticks) is a relatively new phenomenon, the concept of eating delicious sweet treats from sticks has been around for years. Candy lollipops have been enjoyed in various guises for over 300 years, and children have munched on toffee and candy apples for centuries. Sweet delights on sticks came into their own with the invention of the chocolate fondue, where cakes and fruit are dipped into a rich, indulgent chocolate sauce.

In recent years, the latest sweet innovation is cake pops, delicious balls of cake truffle, which can be flavoured and coloured in many different ways, served on sticks and decorated with delicious chocolate or ganache. They can be elaborately crafted into characters, such as bumble bees or frogs. In this book, I have expanded the idea of cake pops to beautiful, mini versions of popular cakes, which are intricately embellished and served on sticks. I have also included a selection of cookie pops, which will never fail to please.

Below Cake pops are not just for children. There is a whole host of sophisticated recipes for adult palates in this book.

Above The classic cake pop is a sponge truffle with a chocolate coating that can be coloured and decorated.

POPS FOR ALL OCCASIONS

Cake pops should, generally, be just one mouthful so that they are easy to eat and your fingers do not get sticky. They are ideal to be served at drinks parties as a sweet canapé, when people need to keep their hands free to hold drinks. They offer great opportunities for some 'wow factor' presentation with creative and dainty decoration. Dusted with edible glitter or topped with gold leaf, your cake pops will literally twinkle and are sure to offer a talking point at any gathering. Let your imagination run wild when decorating – the more elaborate the designs, the more you will delight your guests. The recipes in this book give you ideas for delicious treats for parties, weddings and year-round celebrations, as well as simpler bakes that are suitable for every day – perhaps for lunchboxes or as an after-school treat.

DISPLAYING AND SERVING POPS

There are many ways of serving cookie and cake pops. Cookie pops can be served by laying them flat on platters or serving trays. Cake pops can be more challenging to display and require a little creative imagination, though cake pop stands are now available to buy in specialist cake shops and online. If you are serving cake pops on long thin skewers, you can insert the skewers into polystyrene (Styrofoam) blocks. Or why not display them in vases or tall glasses? If you serve pops regularly, you can make a rack by drilling small holes into a wooden display board. A simple method is to serve the pops on a serving plate or cake stand with the sticks pointing upwards. This is especially useful for heavier pops.

Some cake pops need to be served very soon after being assembled on sticks as the weight of the cake will cause the pops to slip down the sticks if left for too long. The best options to prevent them slipping are either to keep them in the refrigerator until just before serving or, alternatively, to fix a mini or mini mini (extra small) marshmallow on to the skewers below the cakes, which will act as a stopper and prevent the cakes from slipping down the sticks.

You need to be careful when choosing sticks for cake pops given to children – do not use pointy skewers, and collect them up as soon as the pops have been eaten so that they do not become a hazard. (I have seen many a cake pop skewer become a play sword shortly after the cake has been consumed, and I really don't want anyone to be harmed when eating the recipes in this book!)

Above Pops can be shaped and decorated in an endless variety of ways – let your imagination run wild!

'CLASSIC' CAKE POPS

Once you have grasped the basic concept of the classic ball-shaped, truffle-style cake pop, you will easily be able to experiment with other flavour combinations and decoration ideas. If you are short of time, you can substitute ready-made cake into the recipes – store-bought ginger cake or lemon sponge work very well. You will need to use approximately 200g/7oz of ready-made cake as a substitute for any of the classic cake pop recipes in this book.

There is plenty of scope for creativity, so whichever recipe in this book appeals to you, don your apron, pick up your whisk and get popping!

Left There is a lot of fun to be had in making and decorating pops for children's parties.

Ingredients

It is important to buy the best-quality ingredients you can afford, as they do make a difference to the end results. Most of the recipes in this book are made with everyday store-cupboard ingredients. However, there are a few special flavourings that will give your pops the 'wow' factor.

Sugars and icings Giving sweetness to cakes and cookies, sugar comes in many forms. Caster (superfine) sugar is perfect for baking as the crystals of sugar are small and dissolve easily. Soft dark brown sugar is ideal for gingerbreads, whereas soft light brown sugar has a delicate caramel flavour. Muscovado (molasses) sugar is coarser and stickier than dark brown sugar.

Icing (confectioners') sugar is a very fine, powdered sugar that dissolves in water to produce a runny icing that sets. It can be coloured with food colouring. Royal icing sugar is made with egg white and can be whisked to stiff peaks. It is available in powdered form, which requires only water to be added. You can make it by whisking 250g/9oz cups sifted icing sugar with 1 egg white, lightly beaten, and 15ml/ 1 tbsp lemon juice for 3–5 minutes, until it holds stiff peaks. Fondant icing sugar contains glucose and sets with a glossy finish. If you can't get hold of

it, just use icing (confectioners') sugar instead. Ready-to-roll icing is a thick sugarpaste (fondant) that can be used to make decorations or to cover cakes.

Syrups Several types of syrup are used in this book, including golden syrup (or its American equivalent, light corn syrup), honey, maple syrup and rose syrup. Black treacle (molasses) has a strong taste and is used in gingerbreads.

Flours Essential for almost all baking, there are several varieties of flour, including gluten-free flours. Plain (all-purpose) flour is used to make cookies and slices that do not need to rise. Self-raising (self-rising) flour contains baking powder, and is used to make cakes and chewy cookies. If you do not have self-raising flour, you can add 5ml/1 tsp baking powder to 115g/4oz plain (all-purpose) flour, sifting them together. Sift all flours before use.

Raising (rising) agents Baking powder is made from two parts cream of tartar and one part bicarbonate of soda (baking soda). When mixed with liquids and heated, it releases air bubbles, causing baked goods to rise. Bicarbonate of soda is a chemical agent that has a salty, soapy taste, and should only be used sparingly. Yeast is commonly used in breads and dough. It comes in fresh and dried varieties.

Eggs The recipes in this book use large (US extra large) eggs. Always use fresh eggs and, wherever possible, choose free range or organic varieties.

Butter It is best to use unsalted butter in recipes but you can use salted butter, omitting any salt added in the recipe, if you prefer. It is also possible to use margarine or other spreads in cake recipes, though they can give a slightly inferior taste to butter. Always use butter in cookie doughs.

Below Glacé icing can be coloured with food colouring liquids, gels or pastes.

Below Flour should always be sifted to remove lumps before baking.

Below Eggs are used in most cake mixtures and some cookie doughs.

Above Chocolate is an ingredient that never fails to please.

Above Matcha powder will give an unusual colour and taste to cakes.

Above Long shredded soft coconut can be coloured with food colouring.

Cream cheese This is used in cake pop balls and can be added to cookie dough. Some recipes in this book use mascarpone cheese – a soft, thick Italian cheese. You can use low fat versions of both, if you prefer.

Cream Double (heavy) cream can be whipped to stiff peaks and used as a filling in cakes. Sour cream is a thick set cream with a sour taste that can be added to cake mixtures (batters) or buttercreams. You can also make it by adding 15ml/1 tbsp of lemon juice to 250ml/8fl oz double cream, stirring until thick. Crème fraîche can be substituted for sour cream in many recipes. Buttermilk, the residue from the butter-churning process, has a slightly sour taste and can be used in the same way as sour cream.

Vanilla For the best taste, use the seeds of vanilla pods (beans), but vanilla extract or vanilla bean paste can also be used. Avoid vanilla essence as it has a synthetic taste.

Spices Freshly ground spice can transform a recipe. Make sure spices have not passed their use-by dates as they lose strength of flavour over time.

Chocolate The recipes in this book use milk, plain (semisweet) and white chocolate, as well as unsweetened cocoa powder. Chocolate chips can be added to cakes and cookies for extra texture and taste, and chocolate curls (including thin chocolate spaghetti curls) make ideal cake decorations.

Liqueurs A few drops of your favourite alcoholic tipple drizzled over a cake will give a 'naughty but nice' flavour for adults.

Citrus fruits The juice and rind of limes, lemons, oranges and tangerines give a zingy flavour to cakes and cookies. Use a fine zester or grater, and ensure that you do not use the white pith as this has a bitter taste.

Matcha powder is a fine powdered green tea that has a strong and distinctive taste. It gives a quirky flavour, but you only need a little to make an impact, so add it sparingly.

Nuts Many recipes in this book use whole or ground nuts. Nut butters can be added to cakes and cookies, as can almond extract. Be aware that some people suffer from nut allergies.

Dried and candied fruits Sultanas (golden raisins), glacé (candied) cherries, dried cranberries and sour cherries can add flavour and texture to baking.

Coconut This is available in many forms, including fresh coconut, long shredded soft coconut, desiccated (dry unsweetened shredded) coconut and flaked coconut strips.

Decorative ingredients One of the nicest things about pops is the wide variety of decorating options. White chocolate coloured with a few drops of food colouring will make pretty, pastel colour-coated pops. Food colouring gels give a strong colour and blend well with chocolate, but food colouring pastes and powders also work well. For decoration, you can use sugar sprinkles or coloured sugar sand. Applied to melted chocolate or icing while still wet, they will attach firmly when the icing or chocolate sets. Edible lustre spray can be used, together with edible glitter and gold leaf, all of which are available from cake decorating shops. These are lovely for an evening party as they really twinkle under lights.

Essential equipment

You will need a relatively small amount of baking equipment to make the recipes in this book, and you will probably have most of it already in your own kitchen. Although some items involve an initial cost, they really do make baking easier and are a worthwhile investment.

Tins (pans) Many different tins can be used to make pops. It is worth investing in good quality tins that will not rust or distort over time. Loose-bottomed tins have a base that can be lifted out, making it easy to remove the cake. If you do not have the tin called for in a recipe you can use a similar-sized tin, but be aware that the cooking time may need to be adjusted. For example, if you use a smaller tin than stated in the recipe, with the same quantity of cake mixture (batter), it will take longer to cook as the cake mixture will be deeper in the tin.

Silicone cake moulds There is a large variety of silicone moulds available. They can be baked in the oven and cakes literally pop out of them when cooked. They come in decorative patterns and shapes, and are ideal for making mini cakes. If you do not

have the mould required for a recipe, you can bake the cake in a square cake tin and then cut to the size or shape needed. If you are a frequent baker, it is worth investing in some of these moulds.

Mixers and whisks It is useful to have a stand mixer for some of the recipes in this book. While balloon whisks are useful for recipes that do not need much whipping, whisking cake mixtures and cream is much faster using an electric hand whisk or an electric stand mixer.

Sieve (strainer) Essential for sifting flour, cocoa powder and icing (confectioners') sugar, a sieve is an indispensable piece of equipment.

Spatula This is vital for scraping mixtures out of mixing bowls and transferring it into piping bags or tins.

Wire rack Once cookies and cakes are baked, you need to cool them on a wire rack. If they stay in the hot tin or on the hot baking sheet, they can overcook. Let cakes and cookies cool in the tin (pan) or on the baking sheet for a few minutes before releasing them so that they set slightly. This will reduce the chance of them breaking as you transfer them to the wire rack.

Baking parchment and silicone mats A non-stick paper, baking parchment is used to line cake tins (pans) and baking sheets. Always remove the paper before eating. If you bake regularly, you may wish to consider investing in silicone mats (my 'must-have' piece of baking equipment). These are thick mats on which you can cook without greasing. Nothing sticks to them so they are ideal for baking cookies and meringues.

Below Silicone moulds will help you to make your cake pops a uniform shape and size.

Below Basic baking equipment, such as wooden spoons, spatulas and palette knives will be useful for making pops.

Below A wire rack is essential for cooling cakes and cookies once they have been removed from the oven.

Weighing scales Baking is a scientific process, and it is important that ingredients are weighed and measured carefully for best results. Weighing scales are therefore an essential part of your baking equipment kit. For the most accurate quantities use electronic weighing scales as they measure weights to the nearest gram or ounce.

Sugar thermometer This is essential when working with hot liquids where the temperature reached is critical for the recipe, such as marshmallows and some meringues.

Blow torch A chef's blow torch can be used to caramelize sugar and meringue. If you do not have one, it is possible in some recipes to use a hot grill (broiler) instead.

Chocolate dipping fork These are tools used by chocolate makers that enable you to dip truffle centres into melted chocolate or ganache to ensure that the whole truffle is coated. If you do not have one, you can achieve similar results by using a fork.

Below It is worth investing in an electric hand whisk, as it will make short work of beating mixtures.

Above A sugar thermometer is used to make a few recipes in this book, such as meringues.

Piping (pastry) bag and nozzles For effective and neat decoration when icing a cake, best results are achieved when using a piping bag with nozzle attachments. Nozzles come in many different shapes and sizes, allowing you to be wonderfully creative when decorating. The best way to learn how to use a piping bag and nozzle is to make a large batch of buttercream or royal icing, and pipe different shapes using each nozzle to see what results you can achieve.

Below A piping bag and a range of nozzles are necessary for many of the recipes in this book.

Piping bags are available in many forms – waterproof fabric bags that can be reused repeatedly, or disposable plastic bags that are used just once. If you are icing using several different colours it is easiest to use disposable bags, as with a fabric bag you will need to wash and dry it thoroughly between each use. For small amounts, you can make your own piping bags using baking parchment folded into a paper cone.

Pastry (cookie) cutters These come in all sorts of shapes and sizes, and are needed for cutting out cookies.

Skewers and sticks A wide variety of skewers and sticks is available in shops and online. When serving to children you need to remove any sharp points so that they don't cause injury. I have specified the type of stick that I used when I made the recipe, but you can often use any type of stick you like. Check the sticks are appropriate for food use, especially if they are coloured. If you are baking the stick in the oven, you need to make sure the stick is suitable for baking at high temperatures.

Below You can buy all sorts of sticks and skewers, and can colour plain sticks with food colouring.

Tips and techniques

Once you have mastered the basic skills and techniques for successful baking you will be able to create beautiful cake and cookie pops at home. There are a few techniques that will come up time and time again in the recipes, so it is worth getting to grips with them.

Melting chocolate When melting chocolate you need to ensure that all the equipment you use is dry as water can affect the melting properties of chocolate. Break the chocolate into pieces and place in a heatproof bowl. If you are making chocolate ganache, you add the butter and cream to the bowl at this stage. Place the bowl over a small pan containing a little simmering water, ensuring that the bottom of the bowl does not touch the water. Simmer over a gentle heat until the chocolate has melted. Take care when lifting the bowl from the pan as it will be hot and steam will be released; use oven gloves or a dish towel to prevent burns. Alternatively to melt chocolate in a microwave, place the chocolate (and cream and butter, if you are making a ganache) in a microwave-proof bowl and microwave on full power for 1–1½ minutes until the chocolate has melted, stopping every 10–20 seconds to stir the chocolate so that it doesn't burn.

Preparing buttercream The art of a good buttercream is to whisk lots of air into it. This will give a very light and creamy icing that is perfect for piping on to cakes for decoration. To make a basic buttercream, sift 225g/8oz/2 cups icing (confectioners') sugar into a large mixing bowl and add 125g/4¼oz/½ cup of butter. The butter must be very soft otherwise you will end up with lumps. Add 15ml/1 tbsp milk and a little vanilla extract, and whisk using an electric hand whisk or in an electric stand mixer for 2–3 minutes until the mixture is very light, adding a little more milk if it is too dry. Spoon into a piping (pastry) bag fitted with a nozzle of your choice, and you are ready to start decorating.

Whipping to 'peaks' Recipes often call for cream or egg whites to be whipped to 'peaks'. This is easiest in an electric stand mixer or using an electric hand whisk; it can be done with a balloon whisk, but it takes a long time. Place the cream or egg whites in a clean, dry bowl and whisk until the cream or egg whites stand in peaks when you lift up the beaters. For 'soft peaks', the mixture should hold its shape but just flop over slightly. For 'stiff peaks', the mixture should stand firm in peaks. When whipping cream, take care not to over-whip it, as this will cause the cream to separate.

Oven temperatures and times
Every oven is different and therefore the length of time that a recipe takes to cook will vary from oven to oven. You can invest in an oven thermometer which will enable you to check the actual temperature when baking, but the best advice is to get to know your oven. Always check that the item is properly cooked before removing it from the oven, even if the cooking time has elapsed. Cookies should be golden

---

GREASING AND LINING CAKE TINS (PANS)
When baking using tins or baking sheets you need to ensure that they are greased, using softened butter or spray, then lined as shown here.

1 Cut the baking parchment to the size required. For a square tin, snip diagonal cuts at the corners. To line a round tin, cut out a circle of parchment slightly larger than the base of your tin and snip a fringe around the edge. This is easiest with the paper folded into quarters.

2 To line a square tin, place the paper in and fold the edges into the corners. For a round tin, place it in the bottom so that the fringe comes up the sides. Cut a strip of paper the height of the sides and long enough to go all the way round the tin. Place in the tin, smoothing so that it sits over the fringe.

SHAPING AND DECORATING CLASSIC CAKE POPS

The classic cake pop balls are simple to make, and they provide a great base for creative decorations.

1 To prepare cake pops, either make the cake in the recipe, or use 200g/7oz of ready-made sponge cake. Process the cake to crumbs in a food processor. This can also be done by hand, if you prefer.

2 Mix in the ingredients listed in the recipe to moisten the crumbs (such as cream cheese, melted chocolate or butter). It should come together into a paste-like truffle mixture that is fairly firm and not too sticky.

3 Take small pieces of the truffle mixture and form into the desired shape using your fingers. Place on a tray and chill in the freezer for 30 minutes. Once they are firm, press a stick or skewer into each one.

4 Dip into melted chocolate or ganache, making sure the whole truffle is coated. Decorate while the cake pop is still sticky, and then leave to set in a foam block. Store them in the refrigerator until ready to serve.

brown but still quite soft to the touch, as they will set once cool. Cakes should be golden brown and should spring back when pressed with a clean finger. You can also insert a sharp knife or skewer into the centre of a cake to test if it is done. If it comes out clean, the cake is ready. If there is some sticky residue on the knife or skewer, the cake requires a little further cooking.

Caramelizing sugar Use a clean, dry pan when caramelizing sugar. Pour in the sugar and heat gently on the hob. Do not stir but shake the pan from time to time, to prevent the sugar burning. Watch very closely towards the end of cooking as the caramel can burn very quickly. You need to remember that the caramel will keep cooking in the hot pan even after it is removed

from the heat, as the sides and base of the pan are hot, so you should remove it from the heat just before the caramel is ready. If you are using it for sugar work, allow the caramel to thicken for a minute or so before using. If the caramel sets too quickly, simply return it to the heat for a few seconds to melt the sugar again. Take care when working with caramel as it will be very hot.

Below Chocolate can be melted over a pan of simmering water or, for speed, in a microwave.

Below Cream whipped to 'stiff peaks' should hold its shape when lifted up on the whisk.

Below Hot caramel can be drizzled over nuts. When set, they make a lovely decoration for cake pops.

Cake pops

This chapter covers some of the world's most traditional cakes, made into stunning miniature versions and served daintily on sticks. From English classics, such as Mini Victoria Sponge Pops and Cherry Bakewell Pops, to American treats, such as Red Velvet Pops and Whoopie Pie Pops, there is something for every taste. The sticks are inserted into the mini cakes at the last minute, as this will help them to remain perched prettily without dropping.

Mini cupcake pops

Classic cake pops, these dainty mini cakes are ideal for parties. Decorated with icing (which you could colour, if you like) and pretty sugar sprinkles, your guests will not be able to resist these cute cakes. Use different coloured cake cases to add some variety.

MAKES 24

For the cakes
115g/4oz/½ cup butter, softened
115g/4oz/generous ½ cup caster
   (superfine) sugar
2 eggs
75g/3oz/⅔ cup self-raising
   (self-rising) flour
25g/1oz unsweetened cocoa powder
15ml/1 tbsp natural (plain) yogurt

For the buttercream icing
200g/7oz/1¾ cups icing
   (confectioners') sugar
50g/2oz/¼ cup butter, softened
15–30ml/1–2 tbsp milk

To decorate and serve
coloured sugar sprinkles,
   to decorate
24 wooden skewers, to serve

1 Preheat the oven to 180°C/350°F/ Gas 4. Place mini paper cake cases in a 24-cup mini muffin tin (pan). To make the cakes, cream the butter and sugar together until light and fluffy. Beat in the eggs.

2 Sift the flour and cocoa powder into the butter mixture, then fold in with the yogurt. Divide the cake mixture (batter) between the cases; about a heaped teaspoonful in each.

3 Bake for 12–15 minutes, until the cakes spring back when pressed. Transfer to a wire rack to cool.

4 To prepare the icing, sift the icing sugar into a bowl, add the butter and half of the milk. Whisk together for 3 minutes, until light and creamy, adding more milk if necessary.

5 Spoon the icing into a piping (pastry) bag fitted with a large star-shaped nozzle, and pipe a swirl of icing on top of each cupcake. Decorate with sugar sprinkles.

6 Insert a wooden skewer into the base of each cake and display for serving. Depending on the thickness of your cake cases, you may need to pierce the paper cases with a sharp knife before inserting the skewers.

Nutritional information: Energy 125kcal/526 kJ; Protein 1g; Carbohydrate 16g, of which sugars 14g; Fat 7g, of which saturates 4g; Cholesterol 34mg; Calcium 21mg; Fibre 0.1g; Sodium 73mg.

Mini Victoria sponge pops

The Victoria sponge is one of England's most popular teatime treats – light vanilla cakes sandwiched together with buttercream and jam, and elegantly dusted with icing sugar. These mini versions are perfect for serving with a pot of freshly brewed tea for an afternoon tea party.

MAKES 10

For the cakes
50g/2oz/¼ cup butter, softened
50g/2oz/¼ cup caster
　(superfine) sugar
1 egg
5ml/1 tsp vanilla extract
50g/2oz/½ cup self-raising
　(self-rising) flour, sifted
5ml/1 tsp baking powder

For the buttercream and jam filling
100g/3¾oz/scant 1 cup icing
　(confectioners') sugar,
　plus extra for dusting
30g/1¼oz/2½ tbsp butter, softened
30g/1¼oz/scant ¼ cup cream cheese
5ml/1 tsp vanilla extract
a little milk, for mixing (optional)
60–75ml/4–5 tbsp good quality
　strawberry jam

To serve
10 lollipop sticks
10 tiny ribbons (optional)

1 Preheat the oven to 180°C/350°F/Gas 4. Grease a 10-cup straight-sided mini muffin tin (pan) or silicone mould. To make the cakes, cream the butter and sugar together until fluffy. Beat in the egg and vanilla extract.

2 Sift the flour and baking powder into the butter mixture, then fold in. Divide the cake mixture (batter) between the cups of the prepared tin or mould. Bake for 12–15 minutes, until the cakes spring back when gently pressed. Transfer to a wire rack to cool.

3 For the buttercream, sift the icing sugar into a bowl, add the butter, cream cheese and vanilla extract, and whisk together for 3 minutes, or until light and creamy, adding a little milk if necessary.

COOK'S TIP
If you do not have a straight-sided mini muffin silicone mould or tin (pan), bake double the quantity of cake mixture in a greased and lined 20cm/8in square cake tin at 180°C/350°F/Gas 4 for 15–20 minutes. Turn out on to a wire rack to cool. Cut out 10 rounds of cake using a 4cm/1½in round cutter and assemble as above.

4 Cut each of the cakes in half horizontally. Using a piping (pastry) bag fitted with a small star-shaped nozzle, pipe the buttercream on to the bottom half of each cake. Using a teaspoon, add a little strawberry jam to each. Top with the other cake halves and dust with sifted icing sugar. Insert a wooden skewer into the top of each cake and tie a ribbon around it.

Nutritional information: Energy 177kcal/742kJ; Protein 2g; Carbohydrate 24g, of which sugars 20g; Fat 9g, of which saturates 5g; Cholesterol 45mg; Calcium 33mg; Fibre 0.3g; Sodium 136mg.

Orange drizzle pops

Drizzle cake is one of my favourites. A buttery citrus sponge is soaked in citrus juices, which keep the cake really moist and give it an amazing flavour. Decorated with a little white chocolate and topped with sugar stars and edible glitter, these little cakes look as pretty as a picture.

6 Remove the citrus syrup from the heat, then spoon it over the cakes. Leave them to cool in the moulds.

7 When the cakes have absorbed the syrup and are cool, turn out and transfer them to a wire rack set over a sheet of foil or baking parchment to catch any chocolate drips.

MAKES 20

For the cakes
50g/2oz/¼ cup butter, softened
50g/2oz/¼ cup caster
  (superfine) sugar
1 egg
50g/2oz/½ cup self-raising
  (self-rising) flour
finely grated rind and juice of
  1 small orange
juice of 1 lemon
30ml/2 tbsp icing
  (confectioners') sugar

To decorate and serve
50g/2oz white chocolate, melted
yellow sugar stars and edible
  glitter, to decorate
20 wooden skewers, to serve

1 Preheat the oven to 180°C/350°F/ Gas 4. Grease a 20-hole mini loaf silicone mould.

2 Cream the butter and caster sugar together in a bowl until light and fluffy. Beat in the egg.

3 Sift the flour into the butter mixture, add the orange rind, and fold them both in using a spatula. Divide the cake mixture (batter) between the holes of the prepared mould.

4 Bake for 15–18 minutes, or until the cakes spring back when pressed.

5 Heat the orange and lemon juices in a pan with the icing sugar, stirring until the sugar has dissolved.

8 Using a fork, drizzle the melted white chocolate over the cakes. Sprinkle with sugar stars and edible glitter, and leave until the chocolate has set. If it is warm in your kitchen, transfer the cakes to the refrigerator until the chocolate has set.

9 When you are ready to serve, insert a wooden skewer into one of the short sides of each cake and serve immediately.

Nutritional information: Energy 56kcal/235 kJ; Protein 1g; Carbohydrate 6g, of which sugars 4g; Fat 3g, of which saturates 3g; Cholesterol 18mg; Calcium 19mg; Fibre 0.1g; Sodium 32mg.

Red velvet pops

Red velvet cake is an all-time American classic. Dainty cupcakes are coloured red and flavoured with cocoa to give them their distinctive look and taste. Each cupcake is topped with a swirl of cream cheese icing which has a lovely sharpness to complement the sweet sponge cake.

MAKES 20

For the cakes
50g/2oz/¼ cup butter, softened
50g/2oz/¼ cup caster
  (superfine) sugar
1 egg
45g/1¾oz/scant ½ cup self-raising
  (self-rising) flour, sifted
15g/½oz unsweetened cocoa powder,
  sifted, plus extra for dusting
15ml/1 tbsp buttermilk
a few drops of red food colouring gel

For the cream cheese icing
200g/7oz/1¾ cups icing
  (confectioners') sugar
50g/2oz white chocolate, melted
  and cooled
30g/1¼oz/scant ¼ cup cream cheese
15ml/1 tbsp buttermilk

To serve
20 wooden skewers
20 mini marshmallows (optional)

1 Preheat the oven to 180°C/350°F/Gas 4. Grease a 24-cup mini muffin tin (pan). To make the cakes, cream the butter and caster sugar together until light and fluffy, then beat in the egg.

2 Sift the flour and cocoa powder together in a separate bowl, then fold into the butter mixture with the buttermilk and a few drops of red food colouring gel (enough to colour the mixture an even reddish brown).

3 Divide the cake mixture (batter) between 20 cups of the prepared mini muffin tin. Bake for 12–15 minutes, or until the cakes spring back when gently pressed. Transfer to a wire rack to cool.

4 For the icing, sift the icing sugar into a bowl, add the white chocolate, cream cheese and buttermilk, and whisk for 3 minutes, or until creamy.

5 Using a piping (pastry) bag fitted with a large star-shaped nozzle, pipe a swirl of icing on top of each cake. Dust with a little sifted cocoa powder and, when ready to serve, insert a wooden skewer into the base of each cake, securing with a mini marshmallow, if necessary.

Nutritional information: Energy 103kcal/433 kJ; Protein 1g; Carbohydrate 16g, of which sugars 15g; Fat 4g, of which saturates 2g; Cholesterol 20mg; Calcium 22mg; Fibre 0.1g; Sodium 44mg.

Carrot cake pops

These mini cakes are topped with sugar carrots made from ready-to-roll icing and sprayed with edible orange lustre spray. Alternatively, you can colour the icing with a few drops of orange food colouring, or, if short of time, use ready-made sugar carrots, which are available from cake-decorating stores.

MAKES 36

For the cakes
115g/4oz/½ cup butter, softened
115g/4oz/½ cup soft dark brown sugar
2 eggs
115g/4oz/1 cup self-raising (self-rising) flour
65g/2½oz/generous ½ cup walnuts, finely chopped
5ml/1 tsp vanilla extract
5ml/1 tsp ground cinnamon
115g/4oz carrots, peeled and grated

For the cream cheese icing
200g/7oz/1¾ cups icing (confectioners') sugar, sifted
60g/2¼oz/generous ¼ cup cream cheese
30g/1¼oz/2½ tbsp butter, softened
15ml/1 tbsp tangerine or orange juice
a little milk, to mix (optional)

For the decoration
a few drops of green food colouring gel
75g/3oz ready-to-roll white icing (fondant)
edible orange lustre spray or a few drops of orange food colouring gel

To serve
36 wooden skewers

1 Preheat the oven to 180°C/350°F/ Gas 4. Grease and line a 20cm/8in square cake tin (pan). For the cakes, whisk the butter and sugar together until light and creamy. Beat in the eggs.

2 Sift the flour into the butter mixture and fold in with the walnuts, vanilla extract, cinnamon and grated carrots. Spoon the cake mixture (batter) into the cake tin and level the surface.

3 Bake for 20–30 minutes, until golden and the tip of a sharp knife comes out clean when inserted into the centre. Transfer to a wire rack to cool.

4 For the icing, sift the icing sugar into a bowl, add the cream cheese, butter and tangerine or orange juice, and whisk for 3 minutes, or until creamy, adding a little milk if necessary.

5 Trim away the edges of the cake and spread the icing over the top, reserving 30ml/2 tbsp of the icing. Colour this reserved icing green by stirring in a few drops of green food colouring gel.

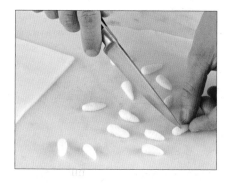

6 Mould the white icing into 36 carrot shapes, press a few lines into each one with a knife, then spray them orange. (Alternatively, knead the orange food colouring gel into the white icing, then shape as above.) Cut the cake into 36 even squares and place a sugar carrot on top of each.

7 Using a piping (pastry) bag fitted with a small leaf-shaped nozzle, pipe the green icing into a leaf shape at the top of each carrot. Chill until the icing is firm. To serve, insert a skewer into the base of each cake.

Nutritional information: Energy 107kcal/450 kJ; Protein 1g; Carbohydrate 14g, of which sugars 11g; Fat 6g, of which saturates 3g; Cholesterol 23mg; Calcium 21mg; Fibre 0.3g; Sodium 49mg.

Banana cake pops

These little cakes take their inspiration from the ever-popular banoffee pie, packed with ripe bananas and a buttery caramel sauce. Topped with a crunchy banana chip, these cakes are sure to be a hit. It is important that you add the lemon juice to the mashed banana to prevent it from discolouring.

MAKES 24

For the cakes
1 banana, peeled
juice of 1 lemon
50g/2oz/¼ cup butter, softened
50g/2oz/4 tbsp soft light brown sugar
1 egg
50g/2oz/½ cup self-raising
   (self-rising) flour
15ml/1 tbsp buttermilk
30g/1¼oz/scant ¼ cup sultanas
   (golden raisins)

For the toffee glaze
65g/2½oz/5 tbsp soft dark
   brown sugar
65g/2½oz/5 tbsp butter
45ml/3 tbsp maple syrup
30ml/2 tbsp double (heavy) cream

To decorate and serve
24 banana chips, to decorate
24 wooden skewers, to serve

1 Preheat the oven to 180°C/350°F/ Gas 4. Grease a 24-cup mini muffin tin (pan).

2 For the cakes, mash the banana and lemon juice together using a fork until you have a paste. Cream the butter and sugar together in a separate bowl until light and fluffy. Beat in the egg and banana paste.

3 Sift in the flour and fold in with the buttermilk and sultanas.

4 Divide the cake mixture (batter) between the cups of the prepared mini muffin tin.

5 Bake for 12–15 minutes, or until the cakes spring back when pressed. Transfer to a wire rack to cool.

6 For the toffee glaze, place the sugar, butter and maple syrup in a pan and simmer over a gentle heat until the sugar has dissolved. Add the cream and whisk well over the heat for a few minutes. Remove from the heat.

7 Invert the cakes so they are wider at the bottom than at the top. Press a banana chip into the top of each.

8 Coat each cake with the toffee glaze using a spoon. Insert a wooden skewer into the base of each cake and serve immediately.

Nutritional information: Energy 82kcal/341 kJ; Protein 0g; Carbohydrate 9g, of which sugars 8g; Fat 5g, of which saturates 3g; Cholesterol 22mg; Calcium 21mg; Fibre 0.3g; Sodium 49mg.

Coffee and walnut pops

Coffee and walnut cake is a popular teatime treat, and these mini versions are a nutaholic's delight. They are topped with coffee buttercream icing and a caramelized walnut that makes them look extra special. If you do not have time to caramelize the walnuts, a plain walnut half can be used instead.

2 Divide the cake mixture (batter) between the cups of the prepared tin. Bake for 12–15 minutes, or until the cakes spring back when pressed. Transfer to a wire rack to cool.

3 To make the caramelized walnuts, arrange the walnuts over a silicone mat or lightly greased baking sheet, leaving a little space between each nut. Gently heat the caster sugar in a pan until it melts and turns a golden caramel colour. Do not stir, but shake the pan from time to time. Watch closely, as the caramel can burn very quickly.

4 Drizzle the caramel over the walnuts using a spoon and leave to set.

5 To prepare the icing, sift the icing sugar into a bowl, add the coffee and the butter, and whisk together for about 3 minutes, or until creamy, adding a little milk if necessary.

6 Using a piping (pastry) bag fitted with a star-shaped nozzle, pipe a swirl of icing on to each cake. Top each one with a caramelized walnut. Insert a wooden skewer into the base of each cake, securing with a mini marshmallow, if necessary.

MAKES 24

For the cakes
115g/4oz/½ cup butter, softened
115g/4oz/generous ½ cup caster (superfine) sugar
2 eggs
75g/3oz/⅔ cup self-raising (self-rising) flour
15ml/1 tbsp instant coffee granules or powder, dissolved in 15ml/ 1 tbsp hot water
50g/2oz/½ cup ground walnuts
15ml/1 tbsp crème fraîche

For the caramelized walnuts
24 whole (shelled) walnuts
150g/5oz/¾ cup caster (superfine) sugar

For the coffee buttercream icing
200g/7oz/1¾ cups icing (confectioners') sugar, sifted
15ml/1 tbsp instant coffee granules or powder, dissolved in 15ml/ 1 tbsp hot water
50g/2oz/¼ cup butter, softened
milk, to mix (optional)

To serve
24 wooden skewers
24 mini marshmallows (optional)

1 Preheat the oven to 180°C/350°F/ Gas 4. Grease a 24-cup mini muffin tin (pan). For the cakes, cream the butter and sugar together. Beat in the eggs. Sift in the flour and fold in with the coffee, ground walnuts and crème fraîche.

Nutritional information: Energy 198kcal/826 kJ; Protein 2g; Carbohydrate 21g, of which sugars 21g; Fat 12g, of which saturates 4g; Cholesterol 35mg; Calcium 15mg; Fibre 0.5g; Sodium 51mg.

Chocolate roulade pops

This delicate roulade sponge contains no flour and is a very elegant cake to serve. Filled with whipped cream and pistachio praline powder, then cut into pops, these taste simply divine. You can use other nuts instead of pistachios, if you prefer – walnuts or pecans work well.

MAKES 24

For the chocolate sponge cake
90g/3½oz/generous ½ cup
  shelled pistachios
45ml/3 tbsp unsweetened cocoa
  powder, sifted, plus extra
  for dusting
100ml/3½fl oz/scant ½ cup full-fat
  (whole) milk
4 eggs, separated
100g/3¾oz/generous ½ cup caster
  (superfine) sugar
icing (confectioners') sugar,
  for dusting

For the filling
50g/2oz/⅓ cup shelled pistachios
90g/3½oz/½ cup caster
  (superfine) sugar
200ml/7fl oz/scant 1 cup double
  (heavy) cream

To serve
24 foil or paper mini cake cases
24 small wooden skewers

1 Preheat the oven to 190°C/375°F/ Gas 5. Grease and line a 40 x 30cm/ 16 x 12in Swiss roll tin (jelly roll pan). For the cake, blitz the pistachios to fine crumbs in a food processor.

2 Put the cocoa powder and milk in a pan and heat for about 3 minutes, stirring occasionally, until you have a smooth paste. Leave to cool.

3 Whisk together the egg yolks and caster sugar until creamy and pale yellow, and the whisk leaves a trail on the surface. Stir in the cocoa paste.

4 Put the egg whites in a clean, dry bowl and whisk to stiff peaks. Fold them into the cake mixture (batter) with the ground pistachios, using a metal spoon. Transfer the mixture to the tin, spreading it evenly.

5 Bake for 15–20 minutes, or until the cake springs back when pressed. Leave to cool in the tin for a few minutes. Place a sheet of baking parchment on the work surface and dust with sifted icing sugar and cocoa powder. Turn the cake out on to the dusted paper, cover with a clean damp dish towel and leave to cool. Remove the dish towel and lining paper, and cut away the crusty edges of the cake.

6 For the filling, arrange the pistachios on a silicone mat or greased baking sheet.

7 Heat the caster sugar in a pan until melted and golden. Do not stir, but shake the pan from time to time to prevent the sugar burning. Pour the caramel over the pistachios, making sure they are all covered. Leave to cool, then blitz to a powder in a food processor.

8 Whip the cream until it forms stiff peaks. Gently spread the cream over the roulade sponge. Sprinkle over the pistachio praline powder. Cut the sponge into quarters so that you have four even-sized rectangles. Roll up each quarter of cake from a long side, using the baking parchment to assist you.

9 Chill for about 2 hours. Cut each roulade into 6 small slices and place each slice in a mini cake case. To serve, insert a wooden skewer into each one.

Nutritional information: Energy 111kcal/463 kJ; Protein 3g; Carbohydrate 5g, of which sugars 5g; Fat 9g, of which saturates 4g; Cholesterol 51mg; Calcium 24mg; Fibre 0g; Sodium 57mg.

Battenberg pops

These Battenberg pops look really dainty on their sticks. To obtain perfect, thin strips of cake, it is best to use a Battenberg tin, which is divided into 4 sections. If you do not have one, bake the pink and yellow cakes in two 20cm/8in square cake tins and cut into thin even-sized strips.

MAKES 36

For the cakes
115g/4oz/ ½ cup butter, softened
115g/4oz/generous ½ cup caster (superfine) sugar
2 eggs
115g/4oz/1 cup self-raising (self-rising) flour
15ml/1 tbsp crème fraîche
a few drops of pink food colouring gel

For the buttercream icing and marzipan covering
185g/6½oz/1⅔ cups icing (confectioners') sugar, plus extra for dusting
30g/1¼oz/2½ tbsp butter, softened
2.5ml/½ tsp vanilla extract
15–30ml/1–2 tbsp milk (optional)
400g/14oz white marzipan

To serve
36 lollipop sticks or skewers

1 Preheat the oven to 180°C/350°F/ Gas 4. Grease and line a 20 x 15cm/ 8 x 6in Battenberg tin (pan).

2 For the cakes, cream the butter and caster sugar together until light and creamy. Beat in the eggs. Sift the flour into the bowl and fold in with the crème fraîche. Transfer half of the cake mixture (batter) to a separate bowl and colour this with the food colouring. Divide the cake mixture into the four sections of the prepared tin (to make two plain cakes and two pink cakes).

3 Bake for 15–20 minutes, until the tip of a sharp knife, inserted into the centre of each cake, comes out clean. Turn out on to a wire rack to cool.

4 For the buttercream, sift the icing sugar into a bowl, add the butter and vanilla extract, and whisk together for about 3 minutes, until creamy, adding a little milk if necessary.

5 Trim away any curved tops of the cakes so that you have four even-sized rectangles. Cut each rectangle in half horizontally, then in half vertically to make 16 long, thin rectangles of cake: eight pink and eight yellow.

6 Sandwich four slices of cake together with buttercream, alternating the pink and yellow slices. This will give you four Battenberg cakes.

7 On an icing sugar-dusted surface, roll out the marzipan to a 3mm/⅛in thickness. Cover the long sides of each cake with a thin layer of buttercream. Cut the marzipan into four pieces, each big enough to wrap around one cake. Roll the marzipan around the cakes, ensuring that the two edges meet on one of the corners. Pinch the join together with your fingers.

8 Chill the cakes for 1 hour. Cut each cake into nine 1cm/½in slices and insert a stick into each slice.

Nutritional information: Energy 123kcal/518 kJ; Protein 1g; Carbohydrate 19g, of which sugars 16g; Fat 5g, of which saturates 2g; Cholesterol 22mg; Calcium 22mg; Fibre 0.5g; Sodium 44mg.

Coconut ice pops

I have a passion for coconut – particularly the long soft shredded variety. It looks particularly pretty when coloured, and has a wide number of uses in baking. Fondant icing sugar is used for the icing. It contains glucose syrup to give it an attractive sheen and is ideal for icing mini cakes.

MAKES 20

For the cakes
50g/2oz/¼ cup butter, softened
50g/2oz/¼ cup caster
   (superfine) sugar
1 egg
50g/2oz/½ cup self-raising
   (self-rising) flour
15ml/1 tbsp natural (plain) yogurt
30g/1¼oz desiccated (dry
   unsweetened shredded) coconut

For the coconut topping and icing
65g/2½oz long soft shredded coconut
a few drops of pink food
   colouring gel
100g/3¾oz/scant 1 cup fondant icing
   sugar or icing (confectioners') sugar
15–30ml/1–2 tbsp coconut rum

To decorate and serve
20 small wooden skewers, to serve
edible glitter, to decorate

1 Preheat the oven to 180°C/350°F/ Gas 4. Grease a 20-hole mini loaf silicone mould (see picture, page 18).

2 For the cakes, cream the butter and caster sugar together until light and fluffy. Beat in the egg.

3 Sift the flour into the butter mixture and fold in with the yogurt and coconut. Divide the cake mixture (batter) between the holes of the prepared mould.

4 Bake for 15–18 minutes, or until the cakes spring back when pressed. Transfer to a wire rack to cool.

5 To make the topping, put half of the coconut in a bowl, add a few drops of pink food colouring gel and stir until it is evenly coloured. Add the remaining white coconut to the pink coconut and mix lightly. Set aside.

6 For the icing, sift the fondant icing sugar into a bowl, add the rum and mix to a smooth icing, adding a little water or additional rum if necessary.

7 To decorate, insert a wooden skewer into one of the short ends of each cake. Partly cover each cake with a little of the icing.

8 Place the iced cakes on a wire rack (with a sheet of foil underneath to catch any drips), sprinkle over the mixed pink and white coconut, then sprinkle with some edible glitter. Let the icing set before serving.

Nutritional information: Energy 82kcal/342kJ; Protein 1g; Carbohydrate 10g, of which sugars 8g; Fat 5g, of which saturates 3g; Cholesterol 17mg; Calcium 12mg; Fibre 0.8g; Sodium 31mg.

Cherry Bakewell pops

These are my version of the popular tarts with almond sponge and almond icing. They look charming topped with a whole, glistening glacé cherry. Almond butter is a thick buttery paste with the delicious taste of almonds. It is available in health food stores and in some supermarkets.

4 Bake for 12–15 minutes, or until the cakes are firm to the touch and golden brown. Transfer to a wire rack to cool.

5 For the icing, sift the fondant icing sugar into a bowl and stir in enough water to give a smooth, thick icing.

6 Place a sheet of foil or baking parchment underneath the wire rack to catch any drips. Invert the cakes so that they are smaller at the top than the bottom. Spoon a little icing on top of each cake so that the icing runs down the sides. Top each cake with a glacé cherry and leave until the icing has set.

7 When ready to serve, poke a stick into the base of each cake, securing with a mini marshmallow, if necessary.

MAKES 24

For the cakes
115g/4oz/½ cup butter, softened
115g/4oz/generous ½ cup caster (superfine) sugar
20ml/4 tsp almond butter
2 eggs
5ml/1 tsp almond extract
75g/3oz/⅔ cup self-raising (self-rising) flour
50g/2oz/½ cup ground almonds
30ml/2 tbsp buttermilk
60ml/4 tbsp cherry or raspberry jam

For the icing and decoration
200g/7oz/1¾ cups fondant icing sugar or icing (confectioners') sugar
45–60ml/3–4 tbsp water
24 glacé (candied) cherries

To serve
24 lollipop sticks
24 mini marshmallows (optional)

1 Preheat the oven to 180°C/350°F/ Gas 4. Grease a 24-cup mini muffin tin (pan).

2 For the cakes, cream the butter, sugar and almond butter together until light and creamy. Beat in the eggs and almond extract. Sift in the flour, then fold it in with the ground almonds and buttermilk.

3 Place a teaspoonful of cake mixture (batter) into each cup of the tin. Top each with 2.5ml/½ tsp jam and cover with a second teaspoonful of the remaining cake mixture.

Nutritional information: Energy 139kcal/585 kJ; Protein 2g; Carbohydrate 19g, of which sugars 17g; Fat 7g, of which saturates 3g; Cholesterol 30mg; Calcium 28mg; Fibre 0.7g; Sodium 53mg.

Whoopie pie pops

An American favourite, whoopie pies are said to have been given their name by Amish farmers who would whoop with delight when they found them in their lunch packs. They are best eaten fresh, so serve them on the day they are made.

MAKES 30

For the cakes
125g/4¼oz/8½ tbsp butter, softened
200g/7oz/1 cup caster
 (superfine) sugar
1 egg
5ml/1 tsp vanilla extract
325g/11½oz/scant 3 cups
 self-raising (self-rising) flour
5ml/1 tsp baking powder
250ml/8fl oz/1 cup buttermilk
100ml/3½fl oz/scant ½ cup hot water
a few drops of pink and green food
 colouring gels

For the filling
225ml/7½fl oz/scant 1 cup double
 (heavy) cream
300g/11oz white chocolate, melted
 and cooled

To serve
30 short wooden canapé skewers

1 First, make the filling, as this needs to set in the refrigerator to be thick enough to hold the pops on the skewers. Whip the cream to stiff peaks.

2 Fold in the melted chocolate and chill for 30 minutes, or until needed.

3 Preheat the oven to 180°C/350°F/Gas 4. Grease and line two baking sheets with baking parchment or silicone mats. For the cakes, cream the butter and sugar together for 2–3 minutes, until light and creamy. Whisk in the egg and vanilla extract.

4 Sift the flour and baking powder into the bowl and add the buttermilk. Whisk again. The mixture will be quite stiff. Whisk in the hot water. Divide the cake mixture (batter) into two bowls. Stir the pink food colouring gel into one bowl of the mixture and the green food colouring gel into the other.

5 Using two piping (pastry) bags fitted with large plain nozzles, pipe thirty 2.5cm/1in rounds of each mixture on to each baking sheet, making 60 cakes.

6 Bake for 10–12 minutes, or until they are firm to touch. Transfer to a wire rack to cool.

7 Using a separate piping (pastry) bag fitted with a small star-shaped nozzle, pipe some filling on to the flat sides of half of the cakes. Top with the remaining cakes. Leave to set, then poke skewers into the filling of each pie to serve.

Nutritional information: Energy 192kcal/806 kJ; Protein 3g; Carbohydrate 22g, of which sugars 14g; Fat 11g, of which saturates 7g; Cholesterol 27mg; Calcium 86mg; Fibre 0.5g; Sodium 108mg.

Key lime pops

The inspiration for these little pops is the American favourite, key lime pie, which comprises a sharp lime mousse in a buttery biscuit (cookie) crumb case and topped with whipped cream. Here I have used cake as the base so they are not too heavy to stay on the sticks.

MAKES 36

For the lime sponge cake
50g/2oz/¼ cup butter, softened
50g/2oz/¼ cup caster
   (superfine) sugar
1 egg
50g/2oz/½ cup self-raising
   (self-rising) flour
15ml/1 tbsp crème fraîche
finely grated rind of 1 lime

For the lime mousse filling
120ml/4fl oz/½ cup crème fraîche
125g/4¼oz mascarpone
juice of 1 lime
15ml/1 tbsp icing
   (confectioners') sugar
15ml/1 tbsp sweetened
   condensed milk
a few drops of green food colouring
   gel (optional)

For the crumb topping
45g/1¾oz/3½ tbsp butter
6 digestive biscuits (graham
   crackers), crushed into crumbs

To serve
36 mini marshmallows
36 wooden skewers
36 ribbons (optional)

1 Preheat the oven to 180°C/350°F/ Gas 4. Grease and line a 20cm/8in square loose-bottomed cake tin (pan).

2 To make the sponge cake, cream the butter and sugar together until light and creamy. Beat in the egg.

3 Sift in the flour, then fold in with the crème fraîche and lime rind. Spoon the cake mixture (batter) into the prepared cake tin and level the surface.

4 Bake for 15–20 minutes, or until it springs back when gently pressed and the tip of a sharp knife comes out clean when inserted into the centre. Leave the cake to cool in the tin.

5 For the filling, whisk the crème fraîche, mascarpone, lime juice, icing sugar and sweetened condensed milk together in a bowl until the mixture is smooth. Add a few drops of green food colouring gel, if using, and mix in until the mousse is a uniform green colour. Spoon the mousse on top of the cooled sponge cake in the tin and smooth it out so that it is level.

6 To prepare the crumb topping, melt the butter in a pan, then remove from the heat and stir in the digestive biscuit crumbs, mixing until the crumbs are all coated in butter. Sprinkle evenly over the mousse, then chill for 2 hours, or until set.

7 To serve, carefully remove the cake from the tin and cut it into 36 equal squares, wiping the knife clean between each cut so that the edges stay neat. Thread a mini marshmallow on to each skewer and place a square of cake on top. Decorate with ribbons, if you like.

Nutritional information: Energy 74kcal/139 kJ; Protein 585g; Carbohydrate 19g, of which sugars 17g; Fat 7g, of which saturates 3g; Cholesterol 30mg; Calcium 28mg; Fibre 0.g; Sodium 48mg.

Apple and cinnamon crumble pops

These pops include all the elements of apple crumble – apple filling, cinnamon and buttery crumble – all wrapped up in little cakes. Whether you have enough willpower to let them cool before serving on sticks will remain to be seen. They normally disappear straight from the oven in our house!

MAKES 24

For the cakes
115g/4oz/½ cup butter, softened
115g/4oz/generous ½ cup caster (superfine) sugar
2 eggs
115g/4oz/1 cup self-raising (self-rising) flour
150g/5oz apple pie filling
15ml/1 tbsp sour cream
5ml/1 tsp ground cinnamon

For the crumble topping
40g/1½oz/3 tbsp butter
65g/2½oz/9 tbsp self-raising (self-rising) flour
30g/1¼oz/2½ tbsp caster (superfine) sugar

To serve
icing (confectioners') sugar, for dusting
24 wooden skewers, to serve

1 Preheat the oven to 180°C/350°F/ Gas 4. Grease a 24-cup mini muffin tin (pan).

2 Begin by preparing the crumble topping. Rub the butter into the flour in a bowl until the mixture resembles fine breadcrumbs. Stir in the caster sugar, then set aside while you make the cakes.

VARIATION
For cherry crumble pops, replace the apple pie filling with cherry pie filling.

3 To make the cakes, cream the butter and caster sugar together until light and fluffy. Beat in the eggs.

4 Sift the flour into the bowl and fold in with the apple pie filling, sour cream and cinnamon. Divide the cake mixture (batter) into the cups of the prepared tin. Top with the crumble.

5 Bake for 15–20 minutes, or until the cakes are golden brown and spring back when gently pressed. Transfer to a wire rack to cool.

6 When ready to serve, dust the cakes with sifted icing sugar, then insert a wooden skewer into the bottom of each cake.

Nutritional information: Energy 109kcal/ 455 kJ; Protein 1g; Carbohydrate 13g, of which sugars 7g; Fat 6g, of which saturates 4g; Cholesterol 34mg; Calcium 34mg; Fibre 0.4g; Sodium 76mg.

Cookie pops

Cookie pops are ideal for children and you can have great fun with the decorations. The cookie pops are baked with the sticks in, so make sure you do not use plastic sticks that will melt in the hot oven! The baked cookies will remain in position as long as you make sure the stick is firmly encased in the dough before they are baked. As well as traditional cookies, this chapter also includes fabulous Iced Yogurt Pretzel Pops, delicate Meringue Pops and beautiful Macaron Pops.

Polka dot cookie pops

Cookie pops are really just an excuse to have an extra large cookie! These pops look very pretty decorated with coloured candy-coated chocolates. They would be a perfect treat to hide in children's lunch boxes, sure to put a smile on their faces when they discover them.

4 Beat in the cream cheese, egg and chocolate chips to make a dough. Divide the dough into 10 equal portions and roll each one into a small ball. Place the balls of dough on the prepared baking sheets, leaving a gap between each one as they will spread during cooking.

MAKES 10

325g/11½oz/scant 3 cups plain (all-purpose) flour
30g/1¼oz unsweetened cocoa powder
5ml/1 tsp bicarbonate of soda (baking soda)
125g/4¼oz/8½ tbsp butter
45ml/3 tbsp golden (light corn) syrup
90g/3½oz/scant ½ cup cream cheese
1 egg, beaten
100g/3¾oz plain (semisweet) chocolate chips
about 60 candy-coated chocolates
10 ice lolly (popsicle) sticks

1 Preheat the oven to 180°C/350°F/Gas 4. Grease and line two large baking sheets.

2 Sift the flour, cocoa powder and bicarbonate of soda into a bowl.

3 Put the butter and syrup in a pan and heat gently until melted and evenly blended. Remove from the heat and allow to cool slightly, then stir into the dry ingredients using a wooden spoon.

5 Press each ball flat using your fingertips, then gently press five or six candy-coated chocolates on to the top of each cookie. Insert an ice lolly stick into the side of each cookie, ensuring that the top of the stick is completely covered in cookie dough.

6 Bake for 12–15 minutes, or until the cookies are just firm. Allow the cookies to cool on the baking sheets for 5 minutes, then transfer them to a wire rack to cool completely.

Nutritional information: Energy 268kcal/1127 kJ; Protein 6g; Carbohydrate 13g, of which sugars 7g; Fat 6g, of which saturates 4g; Cholesterol 34mg; Calcium 34mg; Fibre 0.4g; Sodium 76mg.

Swirly pops

These brightly coloured cookie pops are decorated to look like traditional candy lollipops. They would be perfect for a Willy Wonka-themed party. You can use any colour icing you like – green and red for Christmas, or the colour of a child's favourite football team for a sports party, perhaps.

MAKES 8

For the cookies
115g/4oz/½ cup butter, softened
50g/2oz/¼ cup caster
  (superfine) sugar
175g/6oz/1½ cups plain
  (all-purpose) flour, sifted,
  plus extra for dusting
5ml/1 tsp vanilla extract
15ml/1 tbsp milk, to mix (optional)
8 ice lolly (popsicle) sticks

For the pink icing
250g/9oz/2¼ cups royal icing
  (confectioners') sugar, sifted
15ml/1 tbsp water
a few drops of pink food
  colouring gel

For the white icing
100g/3¾oz/scant 1 cup fondant
  icing (confectioners') sugar, sifted
5ml/1 tsp vanilla extract
15–25ml/1–1½ tbsp water

To decorate
pink and white sugar sprinkles

1 To make the cookies, whisk the butter and caster sugar together until pale and creamy.

2 Sift the flour into the bowl, add the vanilla extract and mix to form a soft dough. If the mixture is too dry, blend in the milk. Wrap the dough in clear film (plastic wrap) and chill for about 1 hour. Meanwhile, preheat the oven to 180°C/350°F/Gas 4. Grease and line two large baking sheets.

3 On a lightly floured surface, roll out the dough to a thickness of 1cm/½in. Cut out 8 rounds using a 7.5cm/3in round pastry (cookie) cutter. Place the cookies on the baking sheets and insert an ice lolly stick into the base of each cookie. Ensure that the top of the stick is completely covered in dough.

4 Bake for 10–15 minutes, or until golden. Leave to cool on the baking sheets for 5 minutes, then transfer to a wire rack to cool completely.

5 For the pink icing, put the royal icing sugar in a bowl with the water and pink food colouring gel. Whisk until the icing is smooth (this will take about 5 minutes). Using a piping (pastry) bag fitted with a small plain nozzle, pipe a spiral of pink icing on to the top of each cookie. Allow the pink icing to set.

6 For the white icing, put the fondant icing sugar into a bowl and stir in the vanilla extract and enough water to make a smooth icing. Using another piping bag fitted with a small plain nozzle, pipe in a spiral pattern between the lines of pink icing.

7 Shake the cookies slightly so that the white icing spreads to completely fill the holes between the pink icing. Decorate with sugar sprinkles, then leave to set before serving.

Nutritional information: Energy 368kcal/1529 kJ; Protein 3g; Carbohydrate 65g, of which sugars 48g; Fat 12g, of which saturates 8g; Cholesterol 31mg; Calcium 38mg; Fibre 0.8g; Sodium 102mg.

Black and white pops

Black and white cookies (also known as half and half cookies) are a popular American favourite. Soft lemon- and vanilla-flavoured cookies are topped with lemon fondant icing and rich chocolate ganache to make these delicious pops.

MAKES 24

For the cookies
175g/6oz/¾ cup butter, softened
200g/7oz/1 cup caster
  (superfine) sugar
2 eggs
275g/10oz/2½ cups self-raising
  (self-rising) flour
finely grated rind of 1 lemon
5ml/1 tsp vanilla extract
120ml/4fl oz/½ cup full-fat
  (whole) milk
24 ovenproof lollipop sticks

For the lemon icing
200g/7oz/1¾ cups fondant icing
  (confectioners') sugar
30–45ml/2–3 tbsp lemon juice

For the chocolate ganache
200g/7oz dark (bittersweet)
  chocolate, chopped
25g/1oz/2 tbsp butter, softened
105ml/7 tbsp double (heavy) cream

1 Preheat the oven to 180°C/350°F/ Gas 4. Grease and line three baking sheets. For the cookies, cream the butter and caster sugar together until light and creamy. Beat in the eggs.

2 Sift the flour into the butter mixture and fold in with the lemon rind, vanilla extract and milk. Using a piping (pastry) bag fitted with a large plain nozzle, pipe 24 rounds of the mixture on to the baking sheets, leaving gaps between them.

3 Insert a stick into each cookie. Ensure that the top of the stick is completely covered in cookie mixture. Bake for 15–20 minutes, until golden. Allow them to cool completely on the baking sheets. Transfer them to a wire rack.

4 For the lemon icing, put the fondant icing sugar in a bowl and stir in enough lemon juice to make a smooth icing. Spread a semi-circle of icing over the top of each cookie. Leave to set.

5 For the ganache, stir the chocolate, butter and cream in a heatproof bowl set over a pan of simmering water, until glossy and smooth. Do not let the base of the bowl touch the water. Set aside for 10 minutes, until cool.

6 Spread the ganache over the other half of each cookie. Allow to set.

Nutritional information: Energy 244kcal/1023kJ; Protein 2g; Carbohydrate 31g, of which sugars 22g; Fat 13g, of which saturates 8g; Cholesterol 47mg; Calcium 57mg; Fibre 0.5g; Sodium 112mg.

Chocolate caramel cookie pops

These cookie pops contain many delicious things – chocolate, fudge and toffee sauce – coated in a thin toffee glaze and decorated with chunks of vanilla fudge. You could decorate with chocolate chips or sprinkles, if you prefer. You can colour plain lollipop sticks with food colouring, if you like.

MAKES 12

For the cookies
125g/4¼oz/8½ tbsp butter, softened
200g/7oz/scant 1 cup soft dark
　brown sugar
275g/10oz/2½ cups plain
　(all-purpose) flour
5ml/1 tsp bicarbonate of soda
　(baking soda)
15ml/1 tbsp toffee sauce
100g/3¾oz white chocolate chips
100g/3¾oz plain (semisweet)
　chocolate chips
12 ice lolly (popsicle) sticks

For the toffee glaze and decoration
200g/7oz/1¾ cups icing
　(confectioners') sugar, sifted
15ml/1 tbsp toffee sauce
60ml/4 tbsp warm water
60g/2¼oz soft vanilla fudge,
　cut into small chunks, to decorate

1 Preheat the oven to 180°C/350°F/ Gas 4. Grease and line two baking sheets. For the cookies, cream the butter and brown sugar together until very pale and creamy. Sift the flour and bicarbonate of soda into the bowl, add the toffee sauce and mix again. Fold in the chocolate chips.

2 Divide the cookie dough into 12 equal portions and roll each one into a small ball. Place the balls of dough on the baking sheets, leaving gaps between them, then press them down with your fingertips or a fork. Insert an ice lolly stick into each cookie, ensuring that the top of the stick is completely covered in cookie dough.

3 Bake for 15–20 minutes, or until the cookies are just firm. Leave the cookies to cool on the baking sheets for about 5 minutes, then transfer them to a wire rack to cool.

4 For the toffee glaze, mix together the icing sugar, toffee sauce and warm water until smooth. Drizzle the glaze over the cookies. Decorate them with chunks of fudge, then leave to set.

Nutritional information: Energy 396kcal/1667kJ; Protein 4g; Carbohydrate 67g, of which sugars 49g; Fat 15g, of which saturates 9g; Cholesterol 25mg; Calcium 76mg; Fibre 0.8g; Sodium 183mg.

Millionaire's shortbread pops

The perfectly combined teatime treat, millionaire's shortbread comprises rich chocolate, sticky caramel and buttery shortbread. These little pop versions would make a popular lunch box or after-school treat, and the stick means that you get to keep your fingers clean while you eat them.

3 On a lightly floured surface, roll out the dough to 1cm/½in thickness. Cut into 12 rectangular cookies. Arrange the cookies on the baking sheets. Insert a stick into the base of each one, ensuring that the top of the stick is completely covered in dough.

4 Bake for 12–15 minutes, or until golden. Leave the cookies to cool completely on the baking sheets. Once cool, transfer them to a wire rack.

MAKES 12

For the shortbread
115g/4oz/½ cup butter, softened
50g/2oz/¼ cup caster
  (superfine) sugar
175g/6oz/1½ cups plain (all-purpose)
  flour, plus extra for dusting
5ml/1 tsp vanilla extract
15ml/1 tbsp milk, to mix (optional)
12 ice lolly (popsicle) sticks

For the caramel
150g/5oz/¾ cup caster
  (superfine) sugar
50g/2oz/¼ cup butter
45ml/3 tbsp double (heavy) cream

For the decoration
100g/3¾oz milk chocolate, melted
coloured sugar sprinkles

1 To make the shortbread, whisk the butter and caster sugar together until pale and creamy.

2 Sift the flour into the bowl, add the vanilla extract and mix to a soft dough. If the mixture is too dry, add in the milk. Wrap the dough in clear film (plastic wrap). Chill for 1 hour. Preheat the oven to 180°C/350°F/Gas 4. Grease and line two baking sheets.

5 To make the caramel, put the caster sugar and butter in a pan and simmer over a gentle heat until the sugar has dissolved and the mixture has turned golden brown. Add the cream and stir over the heat for a few minutes more.

6 Remove from the heat and leave the caramel to cool for 5 minutes. Place a sheet of foil or baking parchment under the wire rack to collect the drips. Dip each cookie into the caramel to coat all over, then place them back on the wire rack to set.

7 To decorate, dip the caramel-coated cookies in the melted chocolate. Decorate with sugar sprinkles and leave to set before serving.

Nutritional information: Energy 244kcal/1020 kJ; Protein 3g; Carbohydrate 25g, of which sugars 14g; Fat 15g, of which saturates 3g; Cholesterol 35mg; Calcium 68mg; Fibre 0.5g; Sodium 114mg.

Gingerbread men pops

These spiced gingerbread men on sticks are sure to delight younger guests. If you are feeling creative, you can pipe on icing clothing, or, if you prefer, you can make large gingerbread men instead. I love the simplicity of these pops with just a chocolate smile and colourful buttons.

MAKES ABOUT 50

120ml/8 tbsp black treacle (molasses)
120ml/8 tbsp golden
   (light corn) syrup
125g/4¼oz/8½ tbsp butter
300g/11oz/2¾ cups plain
   (all-purpose) flour, plus extra
   for dusting
10ml/2 tsp ground cinnamon
5ml/1 tsp ground ginger
5ml/1 tsp vanilla extract
5ml/1 tsp bicarbonate of soda
   (baking soda)
1 egg, beaten
about 50 wooden skewers
50g/2oz milk chocolate, melted
100 mini candy-coated chocolates

1 Put the black treacle, syrup and butter in a pan and heat gently until melted and evenly blended, stirring occasionally. Leave to cool.

2 Sift the flour into a mixing bowl, then add the cinnamon, ginger, vanilla extract and bicarbonate of soda and mix together.

3 Pour the syrup mixture into the dry ingredients and stir well. Beat in the egg. The mixture will be very soft.

4 Leave the mixture to rest at room temperature for 1–2 hours, by which time it will be thicker and suitable for rolling. Preheat the oven to 180°C/350°F/Gas 4. Grease and line three large baking sheets.

5 Roll the dough out to 8mm/⅜in thick on a flour-dusted work surface or piece of baking parchment. Using a gingerbread man cutter, 5cm/2in in height, cut out about 50 men. You can also make different-sized ones.

6 Transfer the gingerbread men to the prepared baking sheets. Insert a skewer firmly into the base of each biscuit (cookie), ensuring that the top of the skewer is completely covered in dough.

7 Bake for 10–12 minutes, or until the biscuits have risen slightly. Leave the biscuits to cool on the baking sheets for a few minutes, then transfer them to a wire rack to cool completely.

8 Spoon the melted chocolate into a piping (pastry) bag fitted with a small plain nozzle. Pipe two eyes and a smile on to each gingerbread man and two dots on his middle for buttons. Press two candy-coated chocolates on to the dots for buttons and leave to set before serving. Add more decorations, if you like.

Nutritional information: Energy 64kcal/270 kJ; Protein 1g; Carbohydrate 10g, of which sugars 5g; Fat 3g, of which saturates 2g; Cholesterol 16mg; Calcium 19mg; Fibre 0.2g; Sodium 40mg.

Honeycomb cookie pops

Always popular with children, honeycomb is the starring centrepiece in these cookie pops. Caramel-flavoured and topped with milk chocolate and extra honeycomb pieces, these cookies are simply delicious! If you want to add little windmills to the sticks, as here, add them after baking.

MAKES 16

For the cookies
350g/12oz/3 cups self-raising (self-rising) flour
200g/7oz/scant 1 cup soft dark brown sugar
5ml/1 tsp bicarbonate of soda (baking soda)
125g/4¼oz/8½ tbsp butter, softened
45ml/3 tbsp golden (light corn) syrup
5ml/1 tsp vanilla extract
finely grated rind of 1 lemon
1 egg, lightly beaten
75g/3oz chocolate-covered honeycomb, chopped
16 skewers or ovenproof sticks (with detachable windmills, if you like)

For the decoration
200g/7oz milk chocolate, melted
75g/3oz chocolate-covered honeycomb, chopped

1 Preheat the oven to 180°C/350°F/ Gas 4. Grease and line two baking sheets. For the cookies, sift the flour into a mixing bowl, then stir in the brown sugar and bicarbonate of soda.

2 Heat the butter and syrup together in a pan until melted and blended. Allow to cool. Stir the cooled melted mixture into the dry ingredients with the vanilla extract and lemon rind. Beat the egg into the mixture, then stir in the honeycomb.

3 Divide the dough into 16 equal portions, roll each portion into a ball and place on the prepared baking sheets, leaving gaps between them as the cookies will spread during cooking. Press each cookie down with a fork and insert a stick into the base of each cookie (removing the windmills, if using). Ensure that the top of the stick is completely covered in cookie dough.

4 Bake for 10–15 minutes, or until golden. Leave the cookies to cool on the baking sheets for a few minutes, then transfer them to a wire rack to cool. Attach the windmills, if using.

5 To decorate, dip about one third of each cookie in the melted chocolate, then sprinkle with the honeycomb. Leave the chocolate to set before serving.

Nutritional information: Energy 301kcal/1267kJ; Protein 4g; Carbohydrate 45g, of which sugars 27g; Fat 13g, of which saturates 8g; Cholesterol 36mg; Calcium 126mg; Fibre 0.9g; Sodium 240mg.

Maple flapjack pops

I love the flavour of maple syrup and it is the ideal sweetener for flapjacks. These little bars are packed full of oats and coconut with hints of cinnamon and vanilla, all enrobed in rich buttery caramel. They are great for picnics as they travel well and do not go soft in the heat.

MAKES 20

For the flapjack
150g/5oz/generous ½ cup soft dark
   brown sugar
150g/5oz/10 tbsp butter
60ml/4 tbsp maple syrup
200g/7oz/2¼ cups rolled oats
100g/3¾oz long soft
   shredded coconut
5ml/1 tsp ground cinnamon
5ml/1 tsp vanilla extract

To serve
20 wooden skewers
20 ribbons (optional)

1 Preheat the oven to 180°C/350°F/ Gas 4. Grease a 30 x 20cm/12 x 8in baking tin (pan).

2 Put the brown sugar, butter and maple syrup in a large pan and heat gently until melted and evenly blended, stirring occasionally. Transfer to a large mixing bowl.

4 Turn the mixture into the prepared tin and press evenly into the tin using the back of a spoon.

5 Bake for 20–25 minutes, or until the top is golden brown and the mixture feels firm when you press it with your finger. Leave to cool completely in the tin.

3 Add the rolled oats, long soft shredded coconut, cinnamon and vanilla extract, and stir well so that all the dry ingredients are covered in the syrup mixture.

6 Remove the cooked flapjack mixture from the tin and cut into 20 even squares. Insert a skewer into each flapjack, pressing the flapjack firmly on to the skewer. Decorate with ribbons, if you like.

VARIATION
You can easily change the flavour of these flapjacks – omit the cinnamon and replace it with the finely grated rind of 1 orange and 1 lemon for citrus flapjacks, or when you remove the flapjacks from the oven, sprinkle over 75g/3oz chocolate chips for chocolate flapjacks.

Nutritional information: Energy 148kcal/620kJ; Protein 1g; Carbohydrate 17g, of which sugars 10g; Fat 9g, of which saturates 5g; Cholesterol 16mg; Calcium 16mg; Fibre 1.2g; Sodium 52mg.

Iced yogurt pretzel pops

My brother lives in New York and when I visit him my favourite treat is yogurt-coated pretzels. This recipe is my pop version and it makes half plain and half yogurt-coated pretzels. If you want to make all yogurt-coated pretzels, double the glaze ingredient quantities.

MAKES 20

For the pretzels
225–275ml/7½–9fl oz/scant 1 cup–
  generous 1 cup warm water
7g/¼oz/1½ tsp active dried yeast
30ml/2 tbsp maple syrup
400g/14oz/3½ cups plain
  (all-purpose) flour, plus extra
  for dusting
5ml/1 tsp salt
15g/½oz/1 tbsp butter, softened

For the simmering solution
2 litres/3½ pints/8 cups water
30ml/2 tbsp bicarbonate of soda
  (baking soda)
salt, to sprinkle

For the yogurt glaze
15ml/1 tbsp virgin coconut oil
30ml/2 tbsp low-fat natural (plain)
  live yogurt
150g/5oz/1¼ cups icing
  (confectioners') sugar, sifted

To serve
20 ice lolly (popsicle) sticks

1 Lightly grease two baking sheets. For the pretzels, place 75ml/5 tbsp of the warm water in a jug (pitcher), sprinkle over the yeast, add the maple syrup and stir well. Leave for 10 minutes, or until a foam has formed on top.

2 Sift the flour into a large bowl. Add the salt, butter and yeast mixture. Gradually add the remaining warm water, mixing until you have a soft but not sticky dough. You may not need all of the water.

3 Knead the dough well either by hand (on a lightly floured surface) or by using an electric stand mixer fitted with a dough hook. Place the dough in a lightly greased bowl, cover and leave to rise in a warm place for about 1 hour, or until doubled in size.

4 Take small pieces of dough (each the size of a small egg) and shape into 20cm/8in long sausage shapes using your hands. It should make twenty.

5 To shape each pretzel, cross the ends of the dough over each other, then twist again and press on to the top of the dough loop, securing in place with a little water. Place the pretzels on to the baking sheets.

6 Preheat the oven to 200°C/400°F/ Gas 6. Prepare the simmering solution by heating the water and bicarbonate of soda in a large pan until hot, but not boiling. Using a slotted spoon, lower each pretzel, one at a time, into the water and leave to cook for 1 minute, then remove using the slotted spoon, drain and return to the baking sheet. Sprinkle the pretzels with salt. Insert a wooden skewer into each one. Bake for 20–25 minutes, until golden. Transfer to a wire rack to cool.

7 For the glaze, heat the coconut oil in a pan until it melts. Add the yogurt and icing sugar and mix well. Remove from the heat and leave to cool for a few minutes. Dip half of the pretzels in the yogurt mixture, then leave to set.

Nutritional information: Energy 115kcal/487kJ; Protein 2g; Carbohydrate 25g, of which sugars 9g; Fat 2g, of which saturates 1g; Cholesterol 2mg; Calcium 32mg; Fibre 0.7g; Sodium 434mg.

Meringue pops

These dainty pink meringues are the lightest of treats and are perfect for an afternoon tea party. I have filled them with chocolate ganache, but you could replace this with rose petal jam and buttercream, if you prefer. Make sure that the meringues are small enough to be just one mouthful.

MAKES 20

For the meringues
3 egg whites
175g/6oz/scant 1 cup caster (superfine) sugar
5ml/1 tsp vanilla extract
a few drops of pink food colouring gel

For the chocolate ganache
100g/3¾oz plain (semisweet) chocolate, roughly chopped
15g/½oz/1 tbsp butter
50ml/2fl oz/¼ cup double (heavy) cream

To serve
20 cocktail sticks (toothpicks)

1 Preheat the oven to 140°C/275°F/Gas 1. Line two baking sheets with silicone mats or grease and line with baking parchment.

2 For the meringues, place the egg whites and caster sugar in a heatproof bowl set over a pan of simmering water. It is important that the bottom of the bowl does not touch the water. Using an electric whisk, whisk the egg whites and sugar together over the heat for 5 minutes, or until they are foamy. Remove the bowl from the heat and whisk the mixture for 5 minutes more, or until the meringue is stiff. Fold in the vanilla extract and food colouring.

3 Using a piping (pastry) bag fitted with a large plain nozzle, pipe 40 rounds of meringue on to the prepared baking sheets.

4 Bake for 1–1¼ hours, or until the meringues are dried and crisp. Leave the meringues to cool completely on the baking sheets.

5 To make the chocolate ganache, place the chocolate, butter and cream in a separate heatproof bowl set over a pan of simmering water, taking care that the bottom of the bowl does not touch the water. Stir until the chocolate has melted and the mixture is smooth and glossy, then remove from the heat and leave to cool for about 1 hour, or until thickened.

6 Using a piping bag fitted with a plain nozzle, pipe a round of ganache on to the flat side of half of the meringues. Top with the flat sides of the remaining meringue halves. Allow to set. Press a cocktail stick into the filling to serve.

Nutritional information: Energy 80kcal/335 kJ; Protein 1g; Carbohydrate 12g, of which sugars 12g; Fat 3g, of which saturates 2g; Cholesterol 5mg; Calcium 4mg; Fibre 0g; Sodium 15mg.

Macaron pops

Macarons are one of life's little luxuries and these are my versions filled with my favourite flavours.

EACH RECIPE MAKES 30
30 canapé skewers, to serve

For rose macarons
125g/4¼oz/generous 1 cup
   ground almonds
175g/6oz/1½ cups icing
   (confectioners') sugar,
   plus 30ml/2 tbsp for the filling
90g/3½oz egg whites (approx. 3 eggs)
75g/3oz/6 tbsp caster
   (superfine) sugar
a few drops of pink food colouring gel
200ml/7fl oz/scant 1 cup double
   (heavy) cream
30ml/2 tbsp rose syrup

For salted caramel macarons
125g/4¼oz/generous 1 cup
   ground almonds
25g/1oz/2 tbsp soft dark brown sugar,
   plus 20ml/4 tsp for the filling
150g/5oz/1¼ cups icing
   (confectioners') sugar
90g/3½oz egg whites (approx. 3 eggs)
75g/3oz/6 tbsp caster
   (superfine) sugar
15g/½oz/1 tbsp butter
a pinch of salt
225ml/7½fl oz/scant 1 cup double
   (heavy) cream

For pistachio macarons
60g/2¼oz/½ cup ground almonds
120g/4½oz/1 cup shelled pistachios
175g/6oz/1½ cups icing
   (confectioners') sugar, plus
   75g/3oz/⅔ cup for the filling
90g/3½oz egg whites (approx. 3 eggs)
75g/3oz/6 tbsp caster (superfine) sugar
a few drops of green food
   colouring gel
15ml/1 tbsp sunflower oil
50g/2oz/¼ cup butter, softened

Rose Macarons

1 Line two baking sheets with silicone mats. Blitz the almonds and 175g/6oz/1½ cups icing sugar in a food processor to a powder. Sift into a bowl. Whisk the egg whites to stiff peaks, then whisk in the caster sugar, a little at a time, until glossy. Add the almond powder, one third at a time, to the meringue mixture with the pink food colouring gel, folding in using a spatula.

2 Using a piping (pastry) bag fitted with a large plain nozzle, pipe 3cm/1¼in rounds on to the baking sheets. Leave for 1 hour so that a skin forms. Preheat the oven to 140°C/275°F/Gas 1. Bake for 20–25 minutes, until firm. Cool on the baking sheets.

3 Whip the cream to stiff peaks. Add the rose syrup and 30ml/2 tbsp icing sugar and whisk again. Using a piping bag fitted with a star-shaped nozzle, pipe a swirl of filling on to the flat side of half of the macarons. Top with the flat sides of the remaining macarons. Insert a skewer. Chill for 2 hours.

Salted Caramel Macarons

1 Line two baking sheets with silicone mats. Blitz the almonds, brown sugar and icing sugar in a food processor to a powder. Sift into a bowl. Whisk the egg whites to stiff peaks, then whisk in the caster sugar, a little at a time, until glossy. Add the almond powder, one third at a time, to the meringue mixture, folding in using a spatula.

2 Using a piping (pastry) bag fitted with a large plain nozzle, pipe 3cm/1¼in rounds on to the baking sheets. Leave for 1 hour so that a skin forms.

3 Preheat the oven to 140°C/275°F/Gas 1. Bake for 20–25 minutes, until firm. Cool on the baking sheets.

4 Put the 20ml/4 tsp brown sugar, butter and salt in a pan and simmer over a gentle heat until the sugar has dissolved. Add 30ml/2 tbsp of cream and whisk over a gentle heat until thick. Cool completely. Whip the remaining cream to stiff peaks, then fold into the sauce. Using a piping bag fitted with a star-shaped nozzle, pipe caramel cream on to the flat side of half of the macarons. Top with the remaining macarons. Insert a skewer and chill for 2 hours.

Pistachio Macarons

1 Line two baking sheets with silicone mats. Blitz the almonds, half the pistachios and the 175g/6oz/1½ cups icing sugar in a food processor to a powder. Sift into a bowl. Whisk the egg whites to stiff peaks, then whisk in the caster sugar, a little at a time, until glossy. Add the nut powder, one third at a time, to the meringue mixture with a few drops of green food colouring gel, folding in using a spatula.

2 Using a piping (pastry) bag fitted with a large plain nozzle, pipe 3cm/1¼in rounds on to the baking sheets. Leave for 1 hour so that a skin forms. Preheat the oven to 140°C/275°F/Gas 1. Bake for 20–25 minutes, until firm. Cool on the baking sheets.

3 Blitz the remaining pistachios and icing sugar in a processor. Add the oil and butter. Blitz to a paste. Spread some paste on to the flat side of half of the macarons. Top with the remaining macarons. Insert a skewer and chill for 2 hours.

Nutritional information (rose): Energy 90kcal/396 kJ; Protein 10g; Carbohydrate 10g, of which sugars 10g; Fat 6g, of which saturates 2g; Cholesterol 9mg; Calcium 14mg; Fibre 0.5g; Sodium 11mg.
Nutritional information (salted caramel): Energy 100kcal/417 kJ; Protein 1g; Carbohydrate 9g, of which sugars 9g; Fat 3g, of which saturates 3g; Cholesterol 11mg; Calcium 15mg; Fibre 0.5g; Sodium 25mg.
Nutritional information (pistachio): Energy 97kcal/408 kJ; Protein 1g; Carbohydrate 9g, of which sugars 9g; Fat 3g, of which saturates 3g; Cholesterol 11mg; Calcium 15mg; Fibre 0.5g; Sodium 25mg.

Party pops

There is something for every party in this chapter, with fun ideas and creative decorations that will delight younger guests. The classic cake pop ball really comes into its own here, with cute frogs, buzzy bees and adorable toadstools. The lovely Alphabet Pops would be great in party bags, thoughtfully decorated with each child's initial. You can use these pops as a base for any decorative design you like – let your imagination run wild! For something simple, Chocolate Crispy Cake Pops and Chocolate Lollipops will never fail to please.

Honey bee pops

These honey-flavoured buzzy little bees with edible rice paper wings are perfect for a teddy bear's picnic or doll's tea party. With honey-infused sponge, enrobed in creamy white chocolate, these little pops taste delicious and look as pretty as a picture.

MAKES 28

For the cakes
80g/3¼oz/6½ tbsp butter, softened
30ml/2 tbsp clear honey
50g/2oz/¼ cup caster
 (superfine) sugar
1 egg
50g/2oz/½ cup self-raising
 (self-rising) flour
15ml/1 tbsp buttermilk
100g/3¾oz/scant ½ cup cream cheese
28 lollipop sticks

For the decoration
a few drops of yellow food
 colouring gel
200g/7oz white chocolate, melted
45ml/3 tbsp icing
 (confectioners') sugar
a few drops of black food
 colouring gel
a few teaspoons of warm water
8 small sheets of edible rice paper

1 Preheat the oven to 180°C/350°F/ Gas 4. Grease and line a 20cm/8in square cake tin (pan).

2 To make the cakes, cream 50g/2oz/ ¼ cup butter, 15ml/1 tbsp of the honey and the caster sugar together until light and fluffy. Beat in the egg. Sift the flour into the butter mixture, add the buttermilk and fold in. Spoon the cake mixture (batter) into the cake tin and level the surface.

3 Bake for 15–20 minutes, or until the cake is golden brown, springs back when gently pressed and the tip of a sharp knife comes out clean when inserted into the centre of the cake. Leave to cool in the tin for a couple of minutes, then turn the cake on to a wire rack to cool completely.

4 When the cake is cool, process it to crumbs in a food processor.

5 Transfer the cake crumbs to a bowl, add the cream cheese, the remaining 30g/1¼oz/2½ tbsp butter and 15ml/ 1 tbsp honey. Mix together.

6 Shape the mixture into 28 egg-shaped balls, each about 1½cm/⅝in in diameter (about the size of a walnut). Place the balls on a tray and chill in the freezer for 30 minutes.

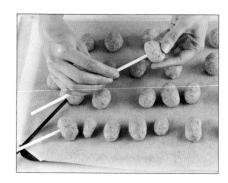

7 Press a stick into each egg-shape. To decorate, whisk a few drops of yellow food colouring gel into the melted white chocolate, then dip each pop into it, coating all over. Press the stick into a foam block. Leave to set.

8 In a separate bowl, mix together the icing sugar, black food colouring gel and enough warm water to make a thick, stiff icing. Using a piping (pastry) bag fitted with a small plain nozzle, pipe thin black lines on to each cake pop for the bee's stripes, then add two small dots for eyes.

9 Cut the rice paper into small wing shapes, each about 2cm/¾in long, then press on to the cake pops using a little of the melted yellow chocolate. Leave to set, then chill until ready to serve.

Nutritional information: Energy 95kcal/408 kJ; Protein 1g; Carbohydrate 12g, of which sugars 12g; Fat 5g, of which saturates 1g; Cholesterol 14mg; Calcium 10mg; Fibre 0.2g; Sodium 40mg.

Frog pops

These cute little pops are as green as can be, with bright green cake inside and a green chocolate coating. If you are having a monster party, you could change the colour of the chocolate to blue or red and pipe wiggly lines of icing for mouths.

MAKES 30

For the cakes
80g/3¼oz/6½ tbsp butter, softened
50g/2oz/¼ cup caster (superfine) sugar
1 egg
50g/2oz/½ cup self-raising
  (self-rising) flour
15ml/1 tbsp buttermilk
a few drops of green food
  colouring gel
100g/3¾oz/scant ½ cup cream cheese
30 lollipop sticks

For the decoration
a few drops of green food
  colouring gel
200g/7oz white chocolate, melted
60 green mini candy-coated
  chocolates

For the buttercream icing
50g/2oz/½ cup icing
  (confectioners') sugar
25g/1oz/2 tbsp butter, softened
5ml/1 tsp milk, to mix (optional)
a few drops of black food
  colouring gel

1 Preheat the oven to 180°C/350°F/ Gas 4. Grease and line a 20cm/8in square cake tin (pan). For the cakes, cream 50g/2oz/¼ cup of the butter and the sugar together until light and fluffy. Beat in the egg. Sift in the flour and fold in with the buttermilk and green food colouring gel.

2 Spoon the mixture into the cake tin and level the surface. Bake for 15–20 minutes, until a knife inserted into the centre comes out clean.

3 Leave for a few minutes in the tin, then transfer to a wire rack to cool.

4 Process the cake to crumbs in a food processor. Transfer the cake crumbs to a bowl, and mix in the cream cheese and the remaining 30g/1¼oz/2½ tbsp butter.

5 Shape the mixture into 30 1½cm/ ⅝in balls (about the size of a walnut). Compress one side of each ball by squeezing to make a flattened area where the mouth will be. Place on a tray and chill in the freezer for 30 minutes.

6 Press a stick into the base of each ball. To decorate, stir the green food colouring gel into the melted white chocolate. Dip in each pop, coating all over, then press the stick into a foam block and leave to set.

7 Fix two green mini candies on top of each frog just after dipping, when the green chocolate has not yet set. Use a small brush to coat the candies in the melted chocolate. Add a mouth line using a cocktail stick (toothpick).

8 To prepare the icing, sift the icing sugar into a bowl, add the butter and whisk until light and creamy, adding the milk, if necessary. Transfer 15ml/ 1 tbsp of the icing to a separate bowl and colour this black with the black food colouring gel.

9 Spoon the two icings into separate piping (pastry) bags, both fitted with a tiny plain nozzle. Pipe small white icing dots on to each of the candies, then pipe a small black dot on top of the white icing to make the eyes. Allow to set completely, then store in the refrigerator until needed.

Nutritional information: Energy 91kcal/379kJ; Protein 1g; Carbohydrate 7g, of which sugars 6g; Fat 7g, of which saturates 4g; Cholesterol 18mg; Calcium 29mg; Fibre 0.1g; Sodium 47mg.

Toadstool pops

Red and white toadstools are one of my best-loved things – we have quite a few toadstool decorations in our cottage and at Christmas our tree is decorated with them too. Needless to say, these adorable pops are one of my favourite recipes in this book!

MAKES 20

For the cakes
50g/2oz/¼ cup butter, softened
50g/2oz/¼ cup caster (superfine) sugar
1 egg
50g/2oz/½ cup self-raising
   (self-rising) flour
5ml/1 tsp vanilla extract

For the decoration
150g/5oz/1¼ cups fondant icing
   (confectioners') sugar, sifted
30–45ml/2–3 tbsp water
a few drops of red food colouring gel
30ml/2 tbsp icing
   (confectioners') sugar

To serve
20 white mini marshmallows
20 wooden skewers

1 Preheat the oven to 180°C/350°F/ Gas 4. Grease a 20-hole mini hemispherical silicone mould (see Cook's Tip). For the cakes, cream the butter and caster sugar together until light and fluffy. Beat in the egg.

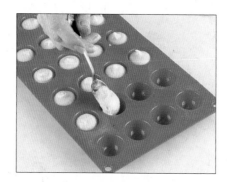

2 Sift the flour into the butter mixture and fold in with the vanilla extract. Spoon the cake mixture (batter) into the holes of the prepared mould.

3 Bake for 10–15 minutes, or until the cakes are golden and spring back when pressed. While the cakes are in the oven, prepare the red icing for decoration. Sift the fondant icing sugar into a bowl and stir in enough water to make a smooth, runny icing. Stir in the red food colouring gel until the icing is bright red in colour.

4 When the cakes are cooked, transfer them to a wire rack and place a sheet of foil or baking parchment under the rack to collect the drips of icing. Spoon the red icing over the warm cakes, making sure that the tops are completely coated. Leave to set.

5 In a separate bowl, mix the 30ml/ 2 tbsp icing sugar with a few drops of warm water until you have a smooth, thick icing. Using a piping (pastry) bag fitted with a small plain nozzle, pipe small dots of white icing on to the toadstools. The red icing must be set before you do this or the icing will run. Leave to set completely.

6 To serve, push a mini marshmallow on to each of the sticks about 1cm/ ½in from the top of the stick. Place a cake on top of each marshmallow.

COOK'S TIP
If you do not have a 20-hole mini hemispherical silicone mould available, you can use a mini muffin tin, trimming the cakes down so that you just use the curved top of each muffin.

Nutritional information: Energy 77kcal/322 kJ; Protein 1g; Carbohydrate 14g, of which sugars 12g; Fat 2g, of which saturates 1g; Cholesterol 17mg; Calcium 12mg; Fibre 0.1g; Sodium 31mg.

Alphabet pops

These cute pops, decorated with letters of the alphabet in bright colours, would be perfect for place setting decorations, or for favours at a wedding celebration showing the bride's and groom's initials. You can decorate the pops in a variety of colours to fit in with any colour scheme.

MAKES 30

For the cake
50g/2oz/¼ cup butter, softened
50g/2oz/¼ cup caster
 (superfine) sugar
1 egg
40g/1½oz/⅓ cup self-raising
 (self-rising) flour
15g/½oz unsweetened cocoa powder
60g/2¼oz/generous ¼ cup
 cream cheese
90g/3½oz plain (semisweet)
 chocolate, melted

For the decoration
200g/7oz white chocolate, melted
various food colouring gels of
 your choice
30 wooden sticks
45ml/3 tbsp icing
 (confectioners') sugar
5–10ml/1–2 tsp warm water

1 Preheat the oven to 180°C/350°F/ Gas 4. Grease and line a 20cm/8in square cake tin (pan). For the cake, cream the butter and sugar together until light and fluffy. Beat in the egg.

2 Sift the flour and cocoa powder into the butter mixture and fold in. Spoon the cake mixture (batter) into the cake tin and level the surface.

3 Bake for 15–20 minutes, or until the cake springs back when gently pressed and the tip of a sharp knife comes out clean when inserted into the centre of the cake. Turn the cake out on to a wire rack and allow it to cool completely.

4 Process the cake to crumbs in a food processor. Transfer the crumbs to a bowl and mix in the cream cheese and melted plain chocolate.

5 Shape the mixture into 30 balls, each about 2cm/¾in in diameter. Place the balls on a tray and chill in the freezer for 30 minutes.

6 For the decoration, divide the melted white chocolate into three bowls and colour each with food colouring gel.

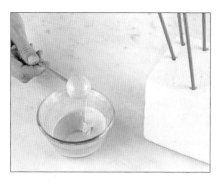

7 Press a wooden stick into each chilled ball. Dip each pop into one of the coloured melted chocolates, coating all over, then press the stick into a foam block and leave to set.

8 Put the icing sugar in a bowl and stir in enough warm water to a make a smooth, thick icing, then stir in some food colouring gel. Using a piping (pastry) bag fitted with a tiny plain nozzle, pipe initials on to each pop. Allow to set, then chill until needed.

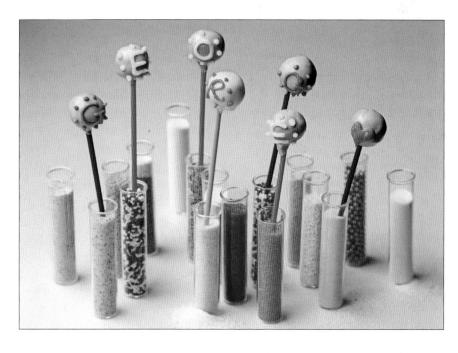

Nutritional information: Energy 39kcal/163 kJ; Protein 0g; Carbohydrate 4g, of which sugars 3g; Fat 3g, of which saturates 2g; Cholesterol 17mg; Calcium 8mg; Fibre 0.1g; Sodium 24mg.

Flowerpot pops

These little cakes, baked in mini terracotta flowerpots, are topped with buttercream and chocolate cookie crumb 'mud'. Decorated with flower cookies and piped icing leaves, they almost look as if they have been plucked from the garden. You can colour the sticks green with food colouring, if you like.

MAKES 14

For the cookie flowers
50g/2oz/¼ cup butter, softened
25g/1oz/2 tbsp caster (superfine) sugar
75g/3oz/¾ cup plain (all-purpose) flour, plus extra for dusting
15ml/1 tbsp rose syrup
about 15ml/1 tbsp milk (optional)
14 ice lolly (popsicle) sticks

For the flowerpot cakes
115g/4oz/½ cup butter, softened
115g/4oz/generous ½ cup caster (superfine) sugar
2 eggs
115g/4oz/1 cup self-raising (self-rising) flour
5ml/1 tsp vanilla extract
15ml/1 tbsp buttermilk
14 paper cake cases
14 new unglazed mini terracotta flowerpots, cleaned and washed

For the icing and decoration
200g/7oz/1¾ cups icing (confectioners') sugar
40g/1½oz/3 tbsp butter, softened
about 30ml/2 tbsp milk
8 chocolate cookies
assorted jelly sweets (candies)
a few drops of green food colouring gel

1 For the cookie flowers, cream the butter and sugar together until light and fluffy. Sift in the flour, add the rose syrup and stir to form a soft dough, adding the milk if it is too dry. Gather the dough into a ball, wrap in clear film (plastic wrap) and chill for 1 hour.

2 Preheat the oven to 180°C/350°F/Gas 4. Grease and line two baking sheets. On a lightly floured surface, roll out the dough to 8mm/⅜in thickness and cut out flowers using a 5cm/2in flower-shaped cutter.

3 Place the cookies on the baking sheets. Insert a stick into the base of each one, ensuring that the top of the stick is completely covered in dough.

4 Bake the cookies for 10–15 minutes, until golden. Leave to cool completely on the baking sheets. Transfer them to a wire rack. Leave the oven on.

5 To make the cakes, cream the butter and sugar together until light and fluffy. Beat in the eggs. Sift the flour into the butter mixture and fold in with the vanilla extract and buttermilk.

6 Flatten out the paper cake cases and press into the flowerpots, smoothing any wrinkles in the paper with your fingers and pressing the cases against the sides of the pots. Using a piping (pastry) bag fitted with a large plain nozzle, pipe the cake mixture (batter) into the flowerpots, filling them to just below the level of the cake case.

7 Place the flowerpots on to a baking sheet and bake for 15–20 minutes, or until the cakes are golden and spring back when gently pressed. Leave the cakes to cool completely in the pots on the baking sheet.

8 To prepare the icing, sift the icing sugar into a bowl, add the butter and milk, and whisk for about 3 minutes, or until light and creamy, adding a little more milk if necessary.

9 Spread the icing over the tops of the cakes, reserving about 45ml/3 tbsp for the leaves. Blitz the cookies to a fine powder in a blender. Press the tops of the cakes into the cookie crumbs to create the 'mud'.

10 To decorate the cookie flowers, put a dot of buttercream on to the jelly sweets and use to decorate the centres of the cookies. Leave to set. Colour the remaining buttercream with the green food colouring gel and, using a piping bag fitted with a leaf-shaped nozzle, pipe two leaves on top of the 'mud' on each flowerpot cake. To serve, poke a cookie flower into the centre of each flowerpot cake between the two green leaves.

Nutritional information: Energy 289kcal/1213kJ; Protein 3g; Carbohydrate 41g, of which sugars 28g; Fat 14g, of which saturates 5g; Cholesterol 53mg; Calcium 50mg; Fibre 0.6g; Sodium 138mg.

Fairy wand pops

You can make these into any shape you wish, such as butterflies, or cut them into round shapes and fill with peppermint dust to make magnifying glasses. Silicone mats are ideal as the sugar glass does not stick to it. If you do not have these, grease the baking sheets with flavourless oil.

MAKES 6

For the cookies
12 cola-flavoured boiled sweets
  (hard candies)
115g/4oz/½ cup butter, softened
50g/2oz/¼ cup caster
  (superfine) sugar
5ml/1 tsp vanilla extract
175g/6oz/1½ cups plain (all-purpose)
  flour, plus extra for dusting
15ml/1 tbsp milk, to mix (optional)

For the icing and decoration
100g/3¾oz/scant 1 cup fondant icing
  (confectioners') sugar
15–30ml/1–2 tbsp water
a few drops of pink food colouring gel
mini mini (extra small) marshmallows
edible silver balls
edible glitter, for sprinkling

1 For the cookies, remove any wrappers from the sweets and blitz them to a fine dust in a blender or food processor. Set aside.

2 Using an electric hand mixer or whisk, whisk the butter, sugar and vanilla extract together until pale and creamy. Sift the flour into the bowl and stir in to form a soft dough. If the mixture is too dry, stir in a little milk. Wrap the dough in clear film (plastic wrap) and chill in the refrigerator for about 1 hour.

3 Preheat the oven to 180°C/350°F/ Gas 4. Place silicone mats on two baking sheets. On a lightly floured surface, roll out the dough to a thickness of 8mm/⅜in. Cut out 6 wand shapes using a card template.

4 Carefully transfer the wands to the prepared baking sheets. Use a small star cutter to cut out a star from the centre of the top of each wand. Fill the hole with a little of the cola dust.

5 Bake for 12–15 minutes, or until the wands are golden and the cola crystals have all melted. Leave to cool completely on the baking sheets so that the sugar glass solidifies.

6 For the icing, sift the fondant icing sugar into a bowl and stir in enough water to give a smooth, thick icing. Stir in the pink food colouring gel.

7 Using a piping (pastry) bag fitted with a tiny plain nozzle, pipe lines of icing around the wands. Decorate with the marshmallows, silver balls and glitter. Leave to set before serving.

Nutritional information: Energy 401kcal/1687kJ; Protein 3g; Carbohydrate 64g, of which sugars 41g; Fat 16g, of which saturates 10g; Cholesterol 41mg; Calcium 51mg; Fibre 1.1g; Sodium 129mg.

Ice cream cone pops

These quirky cakes look exactly like ice cream cones, but the cornets are filled with sponge cake and topped with whipped buttercream, then each one is finished with a chocolate stick. You need to use flat-bottomed ice cream cornets so that they stand upright in the oven.

MAKES 12

For the ice cream cakes
115g/4oz/½ cup butter, softened
115g/4oz/generous ½ cup caster
  (superfine) sugar
2 eggs
115g/4oz/1 cup self-raising
  (self-rising) flour
5ml/1 tsp vanilla extract
12 flat-bottomed ice cream cornets

For the buttercream icing
300g/11oz/2¾ cups icing
  (confectioners') sugar
65g/2½oz/5 tbsp butter, softened
about 45ml/3 tbsp milk

To decorate and serve
6 chocolate sticks and coloured
  sugar sprinkles, to decorate
12 ice lolly (popsicle) sticks,
  to serve (optional)

1 Preheat the oven to 150°C/300°F/ Gas 2. For the ice cream cakes, cream the butter and sugar together until light and fluffy. Beat in the eggs. Sift in the flour and fold into the butter mixture with the vanilla extract.

2 Place the cornets on a baking sheet and, using a piping (pastry) bag fitted with a large plain nozzle, pipe cake mixture (batter) into each one, filling them about three-quarters full.

3 Bake for 30–35 minutes, or until the cakes are golden brown and spring back when gently pressed. Leave to cool completely on the baking sheet.

4 To prepare the icing, sift the icing sugar into a bowl, add the butter and milk, and whisk for 3–5 minutes, or until light and creamy, adding a little more milk if necessary. Using a piping (pastry) bag fitted with a large star-shaped nozzle, pipe a swirl of icing on to the top of each cornet.

5 To decorate, cut the chocolate sticks in half and insert one half into each swirl of icing. Sprinkle with sugar sprinkles. The cone can be the 'stick' for these pops, but you could insert an ice lolly stick into the base of each cake, if you like. Do not do it in advance as the cakes are heavy.

Nutritional information: Energy 319kcal/1342 kJ; Protein 3g; Carbohydrate 47g, of which sugars 39g; Fat 15g, of which saturates 9g; Cholesterol 72mg; Calcium 40mg; Fibre 0.6g; Sodium 123mg.

Jam tart pops

Every year my friend Kathy Brown and I hold an Alice in Wonderland Tea Party. It is a delightful affair and, no matter how fancy the cakes are, the Queen of Hearts' jam tarts are always the first thing to disappear. These mini tarts would be perfect for any party, with a mixture of jams and lemon curd.

MAKES 24

For the tarts
125g/4¼oz/generous 1 cup plain (all-purpose) flour, plus extra for dusting
30g/1¼oz/generous ¼ cup ground almonds
50g/2oz/¼ cup butter, chilled
50g/2oz/¼ cup cream cheese
1 egg yolk
10ml/2 tsp vanilla extract
30g/1¼oz/2½ tbsp caster (superfine) sugar
120ml/8 tbsp different jams and lemon curd

To serve
24 thin pointed wooden skewers

1 Preheat the oven to 180°C/350°F/ Gas 4. Grease two 12-cup mini muffin tins (pans). Sift the flour into a bowl and stir in the almonds. Rub in the butter until it resembles crumbs.

2 Add the cream cheese, egg yolk, vanilla extract and sugar, and mix together to form a soft dough.

3 Gather the dough into a ball in the bowl, cover and chill for 10 minutes.

4 On a lightly floured surface, roll out the dough to 3mm/⅛in thickness. Cut out 24 fluted rounds using a 5cm/2in round fluted pastry (cookie) cutter and press one round into each cup of the prepared mini muffin tins.

5 Spoon 5ml/1 tsp jam or lemon curd into each tart case.

6 Bake for 10–12 minutes, or until the pastry is golden brown and crisp. Slide the tarts out of the tins using a teaspoon and transfer them to a wire rack to cool completely.

7 To serve, insert a wooden skewer into the side of each jam tart and serve immediately.

Nutritional information: Energy 274kcal/311kJ; Protein 1g; Carbohydrate 10g, of which sugars 5g; Fat 4g, of which saturates 2g; Cholesterol 15mg; Calcium 14mg; Fibre 0.4g; Sodium 22mg.

Pina colada marshmallow swirly pops

Making homemade marshmallow may take a little extra effort but the results are far superior to store-bought marshmallows. They can be made with almost any flavour you like. I have made these with pineapple and coconut – flavours that transport me to sunny climes and tropical beaches!

MAKES 15

For the setting paste
75ml/5 tbsp pineapple juice
50ml/2fl oz/¼ cup coconut milk
25g/1oz powdered gelatine

For the syrup
500g/1¼lb/2½ cups caster
    (superfine) sugar
60ml/4 tbsp golden (light corn) syrup
250ml/8fl oz/1 cup pineapple juice
60ml/4 tbsp coconut rum
a few drops of yellow food
    colouring gel
plenty of icing (confectioners')
    sugar, sifted, for dusting

To serve
15 lollipop sticks

1 To prepare the setting paste, whisk the pineapple juice, coconut milk and gelatine together in the bowl of an electric stand mixer. Set aside.

2 For the syrup, place the caster sugar, syrup, pineapple juice and rum in a heavy pan and simmer over a gentle heat until the sugar has dissolved. Turn up the heat and boil the mixture until it reaches the hard ball stage (130°C/266°F on a sugar thermometer).

3 Turn the stand mixer on and whisk the setting paste, then, with the mixer whisking constantly, pour in the hot syrup in a thin steady stream and whisk for 10–15 minutes, or until the mixture becomes white, thick and meringue-like.

4 Line a 30 x 20cm/12 x 8in shallow-sided roasting tin (pan) with a layer of clear film (plastic wrap) or with a silicone mat. Pour half of the marshmallow mixture into the tin so that it covers the whole of the bottom of the tin.

5 Stir the yellow food colouring gel into the remaining marshmallow, mixing to a uniform yellow colour. Pour the yellow marshmallow on top of the white marshmallow, then leave to set for 2 hours.

6 Dust the top of the marshmallow with icing sugar, invert it on to a flat surface and gently remove the clear film, dusting the edge that is being pulled away from the clear film with icing sugar to absorb the stickiness. Dust again with icing sugar.

7 Cut 1cm/½in-wide long strips of the marshmallow using icing sugar-dusted scissors, dusting the exposed cut sides with a little icing sugar. Roll up the strips into spirals so that the stripes are visible. Secure each with a stick.

Nutritional information: Energy 186kcal/794kJ; Protein 1g; Carbohydrate 47g, of which sugars 47g; Fat 0g, of which saturates 0g; Cholesterol 0mg; Calcium 11mg; Fibre 0g; Sodium 23mg.

Chocolate crispy cake pops

This recipe is easy to make and perfect for allowing little hands to help at the mixing stage.
You can make these pops either large or small. You can colour the sticks with edible food colouring
or buy coloured ones from cake or craft stores, but do check they are suitable for food use first.

MAKES 8 LARGE OR 18 SMALL

For the crispy cakes
30ml/2 tbsp golden
  (light corn) syrup
60g/2¼oz/4½ tbsp butter
60g/2¼oz white chocolate,
  roughly chopped
90g/3½oz crisped rice cereal
50g/2oz/⅓ cup mixed dried fruit,
  such as sultanas (golden raisins),
  cranberries and raisins

To decorate
popping candy and sprinkles

To serve
8 or 18 ice lolly (popsicle) sticks

1 Put the syrup, butter and white chocolate in a pan and heat gently, stirring constantly, until melted and blended. Transfer to a mixing bowl.

2 Stir in the rice cereal and dried fruit and mix well to coat everything in the syrup mixture.

3 To make large crispy pops, divide the mixture into 8 portions and press each portion into a 7.5cm/3in round chef's ring or biscuit (cookie) cutter placed on a sheet of foil. Press an ice lolly stick into each one. Sprinkle with popping candy and sugar sprinkles, and leave to set before serving.

4 To make smaller crispy pops, lightly grease two mini cupcake tins (pans) and press the mixture into 18 of the cups to shape. Leave to set for about 10 minutes.

5 Turn the crispy cakes out on to a sheet of baking parchment to catch any sprinkles, then decorate with popping candy and sprinkles. Press an ice lolly stick into each one and allow to set completely before serving.

Nutritional information (large): Energy 167kcal/698kJ; Protein 2g; Carbohydrate 23g, of which sugars 14g; Fat 9g, of which saturates 5g; Cholesterol 16mg; Calcium 79mg; Fibre 0.5g; Sodium 140mg.
Nutritional information (small): Energy 74kcal/310kJ; Protein 1g; Carbohydrate 10g, of which sugars 6g; Fat 4g, of which saturates 2g; Cholesterol 7mg; Calcium 35mg; Fibre 0.2g; Sodium 62mg.

Chocolate lollipops

These chocolate lollipops are so easy to prepare and make a special treat. Topped with dried cranberries and bright green pistachios, they look really enticing. You can use milk chocolate, if you prefer. If your kitchen is warm, it may be necessary to put them in the refrigerator to set.

MAKES 6

100g/3¾oz plain (semisweet)
   chocolate, melted
100g/3¾oz white chocolate, melted
6 ice lolly (popsicle) sticks
30g/1¼oz/scant ¼ cup
   dried cranberries
30g/1¼oz/scant ¼ cup dried
   sour cherries
60g/2¼oz/generous ½ cup mixed nuts

1 Lay a silicone mat on a baking sheet. Allow the melted chocolate to cool and thicken slightly, then spread out three plain chocolate discs and three white chocolate discs on the baking sheet.

2 Insert an ice lolly stick into an edge of each round, making sure that it is completely covered in chocolate.

3 Sprinkle each disc with the dried cranberries, dried sour cherries and mixed nuts, then leave to set completely before carefully removing them from the silicone mats to serve.

VARIATION
If you do not like dried fruit and nuts, you can omit these from the recipe. Make plain and white chocolate discs following the recipe above, then melt an additional 100g/3¾oz white chocolate, divide it into two bowls and colour each with a few drops of food colouring gel of your choice. Drizzle lines of the coloured chocolates in patterns over the discs and leave to set.

Nutritional information: Energy 241kcal/1009 kJ; Protein 5g; Carbohydrate 23g, of which sugars 22g; Fat 15g, of which saturates 7g; Cholesterol 1mg; Calcium 64mg; Fibre 2.7g; Sodium 50mg.

Rich and indulgent pops

When only a real treat will do, this chapter is full of mouthwatering options. There is plenty to tempt grown-up tastebuds, with flavourings like coffee, matcha green tea, amaretto, mint and chilli, as well as a medley of chocolate delights, such as Rocky Road Pops and Chocolate Mud Pie Pops. The sticks mean that fingers are kept clean, which is perfect for gooey morsels such as Sticky Toffee Pudding Pops and Lemon Profiterole Pops.

Baked Alaskas

With hot meringue and ice-cold ice cream, baked Alaska is a perfect summertime dessert. You need to serve these little cakes straightaway so that the ice cream is still frozen, to give your guests the hot-cold sensation of glorious baked Alaska.

MAKES 12

For the cake and ice cream
115g/4oz/½ cup butter, softened
115g/4oz/generous ½ cup caster
   (superfine) sugar
2 eggs
115g/4oz/1 cup self-raising
   (self-rising) flour
5ml/1 tsp vanilla extract
about 90ml/6 tbsp vanilla ice cream
   (not soft-scoop)

For the meringue
60ml/4 tbsp water
200g/7oz/1 cup caster
   (superfine) sugar
5ml/1 tsp vanilla extract
2 egg whites

To serve
12 paper or foil cake cases
12 thin-handled plastic spoons

1 Preheat the oven to 180°C/350°F/ Gas 4. Grease a 20cm/8in square cake tin (pan). For the cake, cream the butter and sugar until light and fluffy. Beat in the eggs. Sift in the flour and fold in with the vanilla extract.

2 Spoon the cake mixture (batter) into the prepared cake tin and level the surface. Bake for 20–25 minutes, or until the cake is golden and springs back when gently pressed. Turn the cake out on to a wire rack to cool.

3 Transfer the cake to a clean work surface and cut out 12 rounds of cake using a 3cm/1¼in round cutter. Scoop out the middle of each small cake using a melon baller to make a dip for the ice cream to sit in. Make 12 melon ball scoops of ice cream, place them on a tray and return to the freezer so that they are very firm.

4 For the meringue, put the water, sugar and vanilla extract in a pan and simmer until the sugar has dissolved. Bring to the boil and boil until it reaches soft ball stage (114°C/238°F on a sugar thermometer).

5 In an electric stand mixer, whisk the egg whites to stiff peaks, then gradually add the hot syrup in a thin drizzle, whisking constantly. Whisk until the meringue mixture cools; about 10–15 minutes.

6 Spoon the meringue mixture into a piping (pastry) bag fitted with a large plain nozzle. Place 12 cake cases on a tray and press them out flat. Place each cake on a flattened cake case. Pipe a thick ring of meringue around the sides of each cake and spread out evenly using a round-bladed knife to cover the sides completely.

7 Place a ball of ice cream in the hole on the top of each cake. Working quickly, pipe meringue on top of each Alaska to cover the ice cream and cake completely. Use a chef's blowtorch to caramelize the meringue and insert spoons in the tops. Serve immediately.

Nutritional information: Energy 237kcal/996kJ; Protein 3g; Carbohydrate 36g, of which sugars 29g; Fat 10g, of which saturates 6g; Cholesterol 61mg; Calcium 52mg; Fibre 0.4g; Sodium 127mg.

Baked cheesecake pops

Baked cheesecake, rich and creamy, makes a divine sweet canapé. It can be prepared ahead of time so it is ideal when you are catering for large numbers. To serve, just dust with icing sugar, cut into slices and secure on a stick. It is best to insert the stick at the last minute, just before serving.

MAKES 25

For the cheesecake
250g/9oz/1⅛ cups cream cheese
finely grated rind of 1 lemon and
   1 lime
100g/3¾oz/generous ½ cup caster
   (superfine) sugar
2 eggs
5ml/1 tsp vanilla extract
250ml/8fl oz/1 cup crème fraîche
60g/2¼oz/generous ½ cup
   self-raising (self-rising) flour
icing (confectioners') sugar,
   for dusting

To serve
25 mini paper cake cases
25 lollipop sticks

1 Preheat the oven to 180°C/350°F/ Gas 4. Grease and line a 20cm/8in loose-bottomed square cake tin (pan).

2 Put the cream cheese, citrus rinds, caster sugar, eggs, vanilla extract, crème fraîche and flour in a bowl and whisk together until you have a smooth, creamy mixture.

3 Pour the cheesecake mixture evenly into the prepared cake tin.

4 Bake for 40–50 minutes, or until the top is golden brown and wobbles very slightly when shaken gently. Leave to cool completely in the tin.

5 Carefully remove the cheesecake from the tin. Cut it into 25 small rectangles and dust with icing sugar.

6 Chill the cheesecakes in the refrigerator until you are ready to serve. Before serving, insert a stick through a mini paper case, then into the bottom of the cheesecake rectangle, so that the cheesecake sits in the paper case when you hold the stick upright.

Nutritional information: Energy 112kcal/466kJ; Protein 1g; Carbohydrate 6g, of which sugars 4g; Fat 9g, of which saturates 6g; Cholesterol 40mg; Calcium 27mg; Fibre 0.1g; Sodium 48mg.

Rocky road pops

These pops take their inspiration from rocky road ice cream and are packed with cherries, chocolate and marshmallows. I have added a crunch of two types of cookies for an extra special treat. You only need to cut small squares of this slice for each pop as the mixture is very rich.

MAKES 28

For the chocolate slice
400g/14oz plain (semisweet) chocolate, chopped
125g/4¼oz/8½ tbsp butter
100g/3¾oz/scant 2 cups digestive biscuits (graham crackers), crushed
100g/3¾oz/scant 2 cups chocolate sandwich cookies, crushed
75g/3oz mini marshmallows
150g/5oz/scant ¾ cup glacé (candied) cherries, halved

For the topping
100g/3¾oz/scant ½ cup glacé (candied) cherries, halved
50g/2oz mini marshmallows
100g/3¾oz white chocolate, melted

To serve
28 wooden skewers

1 Grease and line a 28 x 18cm/11 x 7in deep rectangular cake tin (pan).

2 To make the chocolate slice, place the chocolate and butter in a large heatproof bowl set over a pan of simmering water, taking care that the water does not touch the bottom of the bowl. Stir until the butter and chocolate are melted and blended, then remove from the heat.

3 Add all the remaining ingredients for the chocolate slice to the bowl and mix well to coat everything in the chocolate.

4 Spoon the mixture into the tin and press out flat using a spoon.

5 For the topping, sprinkle the glacé cherries and mini marshmallows over the top. Drizzle over the white chocolate in thin lines using a spoon. Leave to set in the refrigerator.

6 To serve, remove the slice from the tin and cut into 28 squares. Insert a wooden skewer into each square.

Nutritional information: Energy 196kcal/821kJ; Protein 2g; Carbohydrate 26g, of which sugars 22g; Fat 10g, of which saturates 6g; Cholesterol 14mg; Calcium 27mg; Fibre 0.3g; Sodium 62mg.

Black Forest cherry pops

The German Black Forest gateau is one of my favourite cakes. These mini versions would make a fun canapé to serve at any party. For me, the best topping for these little cakes is whipped cream from a spray can, but you can replace this with cream whipped by hand, if you prefer.

MAKES 30

For the cakes
115g/4oz/½ cup butter, softened
115g/4oz/generous ½ cup caster
  (superfine) sugar
2 eggs
115g/4oz/1 cup self-raising
  (self-rising) flour
2.5ml/½ tsp vanilla extract
90g/3½oz cherry compote
75ml/2½fl oz/⅓ cup low-fat natural
  (plain) yogurt

For the chocolate ganache
200g/7oz plain (semisweet)
  chocolate, chopped
105ml/7 tbsp double (heavy) cream
25g/1oz/2 tbsp butter, softened

To decorate and serve
a spray can of whipped cream
30 fresh cherries
chocolate 'spaghetti' curls, to sprinkle
30 lollipop sticks, to serve

1 Preheat the oven to 180°C/350°F/ Gas 4. Grease a 30-cup mini muffin tin (pan).

2 For the cakes, cream the butter and sugar together until light and fluffy. Beat in the eggs. Sift in the flour and fold in with the vanilla extract, cherry compote and yogurt. Divide the cake mixture (batter) between the cups of the prepared tin; about a heaped teaspoon in each.

3 Bake for 15–18 minutes, until the cakes spring back when pressed. Transfer to a wire rack to cool.

4 Once cool, insert a stick into the base of each cake.

5 To prepare the chocolate ganache, place the chocolate, cream and butter in a heatproof bowl set over a pan of simmering water, taking care that the water does not touch the bottom of the bowl. Stir until you have a smooth, glossy sauce. Remove from the heat.

6 Dip the top of each cake into the chocolate ganache, then insert the sticks into a foam block and leave the cake pops to set.

7 When you are ready to serve, squirt a little spray cream on to the top of each cake, top with a whole cherry and sprinkle with chocolate spaghetti curls.

Nutritional information: Energy 150kcal/624kJ; Protein 2g; Carbohydrate 13g, of which sugars 10g; Fat 10g, of which saturates 6g; Cholesterol 36mg; Calcium 29mg; Fibre 0.2g; Sodium 52mg.

Peanut butter pops

I love the combination of peanut butter and chocolate – the salty peanut and smooth chocolate just melt in the mouth, giving the perfect sweet and savoury combination. Here, a peanut butter sponge is coated in melted chocolate and topped with chopped honey-roasted peanuts.

5 Process the cooled cake to crumbs in a food processor. Transfer the cake crumbs to a bowl, add the remaining peanut butter, the cream cheese and chocolate chips and mix together.

6 Shape the mixture into 28 even-sized balls (about the size of walnuts). Place the balls on a tray and chill in the freezer for 30 minutes.

7 Remove the balls from the freezer and press a wooden skewer into each one.

8 To decorate, dip each ball into the melted chocolate, coating all over, then dip the tops into the chopped peanuts. Press the wooden skewers into a foam block and leave to set, then chill in the refrigerator until you are ready to serve.

MAKES 28

For the cakes
50g/2oz/¼ cup butter, softened
50g/2oz/¼ cup caster
  (superfine) sugar
45ml/3 tbsp peanut butter
1 egg
50g/2oz/½ cup self-raising
  (self-rising) flour
100g/3¾oz/scant ½ cup cream cheese
50g/2oz plain (semisweet)
  chocolate chips
28 wooden skewers

For the decoration
300g/11oz plain (semisweet)
  chocolate, melted
75g/3oz/¾ cup honey-roasted
  peanuts, finely chopped

1 Preheat the oven to 180°C/350°F/ Gas 4. Grease and line a 20cm/8in square cake tin (pan).

2 For the cakes, cream the butter, caster sugar and 25ml/1½ tbsp of the peanut butter together in a bowl until light and fluffy. Beat in the egg.

3 Sift the flour into the bowl and fold into the butter mixture. Spoon the cake mixture (batter) into the prepared tin and level the surface.

4 Bake for 15–20 minutes, until the cake is golden and the tip of a sharp knife comes out clean when inserted into the centre of the cake. Turn out on to a wire rack to cool.

Nutritional information: Energy 127kcal/529kJ; Protein 2g; Carbohydrate 11g, of which sugars 10g; Fat 9g, of which saturates 5g; Cholesterol 16mg; Calcium 11mg; Fibre 0.3g; Sodium 31mg.

Sticky toffee pudding pops

Classic sticky toffee pudding is a delicious toffee-flavoured sponge pudding, studded with dates and topped with a sticky toffee sauce. These gooey mini toffee cakes, topped with clotted cream and a thin slice of date, can be served warm for an extra-special treat.

MAKES 24

For the cakes
115g/4oz/½ cup butter, softened
115g/4oz/½ cup soft dark
   brown sugar
2 eggs
115g/4oz/1 cup self-raising
   (self-rising) flour
15ml/1 tbsp buttermilk
90g/3½oz/generous ½ cup stoned
   (pitted) dates

For the toffee sauce
60ml/4 tbsp soft dark brown sugar
40g/1½oz/3 tbsp butter
a pinch of salt
90ml/6 tbsp double (heavy) cream

To decorate and serve
24 lollipop sticks, to serve
60ml/4 tbsp clotted or whipped
   cream, to decorate

1 Preheat the oven to 180°C/350°F/
Gas 4. Grease a 24-cup mini muffin
tin (pan). To make the cakes, cream
the butter and brown sugar together
until light and fluffy. Beat in the eggs.

2 Sift in the flour and fold into the
butter mixture with the buttermilk.
Chop 60g/2¼oz/⅓ cup of the dates
into very small pieces and stir into
the cake mixture (batter). Divide the
cake mixture between the cups of
the mini muffin tin.

3 Bake for 12–15 minutes, or until
the cakes are golden and spring
back when gently pressed. Transfer
to a wire rack to cool.

4 Slice the remaining dates into 24
thin slices and set aside. For the
toffee sauce, put the sugar, butter
and salt in a pan and heat until the
butter has melted and the sugar has
dissolved, stirring. Stir in the cream
and simmer over a gentle heat until
thickened. Allow to cool slightly.

5 Insert a stick into the base of each
cake and dip the top of each cake
into the toffee sauce.

6 Top each cake with 2.5ml/½ tsp
clotted cream and decorate each
with one of the reserved date slices.
Serve immediately.

Nutritional information: Energy 137kcal/574kJ; Protein 1g; Carbohydrate 14g, of which sugars 10g; Fat 9g, of which saturates 5g; Cholesterol 41mg; Calcium 28mg; Fibre 0.5g; Sodium 82mg.

Lemon profiterole pops

Delicate choux pastry is enjoyed by people all over the world, with chocolate profiteroles as a popular classic. These profiterole pops are slightly more unusual but no less delicious, with a tangy lemon curd cream filling and sharp lemon icing, topped with a sugary lemon jelly slice.

MAKES 30

For the choux pastry
65g/2½oz/9 tbsp plain
    (all-purpose) flour
150ml/¼ pint/⅔ cup water
50g/2oz/¼ cup butter
2 eggs, beaten
finely grated rind of 1 lemon

For the filling
200ml/7fl oz/scant 1 cup double
    (heavy) cream
30ml/2 tbsp lemon curd

For the icing
200g/7oz/1¾ cups fondant icing
    (confectioners') sugar, sifted
juice of 1 lemon
a few drops of yellow food
    colouring gel (optional)

To decorate and serve
30 jelly lemon slices, to decorate
30 wooden skewers, to serve

1 Preheat the oven to 200°C/400°F/ Gas 6. Grease and line two large baking sheets.

2 For the choux pastry, sift the flour twice into a bowl to remove all lumps and add as much air as possible.

3 Place the water and butter in a pan and heat gently until the butter has melted. Bring to the boil, then quickly add all the flour in one go and remove from the heat. Beat the mixture hard with a wooden spoon until it forms a ball and no longer sticks to the sides of the pan. Leave to cool for about 5 minutes.

4 Whisk in the beaten eggs, a little at a time, using a balloon whisk and beating well between each addition. Whisk in the lemon rind. The mixture will form a sticky paste that holds its shape when you lift the whisk up.

5 Using a piping (pastry) bag fitted with a large plain nozzle, pipe 30 small balls of the pastry on to the baking sheets. Wet your finger and smooth down any peaks from the piping so that the pastry is smooth.

6 Bake for 12 minutes, then remove from the oven and, using a sharp knife, cut a small slit in the side of each bun to allow the steam to escape, then return to the oven for a further 2–5 minutes, or until crisp. Transfer to a wire rack to cool.

7 For the filling, whip the cream in a bowl until it forms stiff peaks, then fold in the lemon curd. Make the slit in each choux bun slightly wider. Using another piping bag fitted with the same size nozzle, pipe some filling into each bun through the slit.

8 For the icing, put the fondant icing sugar in a bowl and stir in enough lemon juice to make a smooth, thick icing. Stir in a few drops of yellow food colouring gel, if you wish.

9 Spread the lemon icing over the top of each profiterole and top with a jelly lemon slice to decorate. Leave the icing to set. To serve, insert a wooden skewer into the base of each profiterole and serve immediately.

Nutritional information: Energy 88kcal/367kJ; Protein 1g; Carbohydrate 9g, of which sugars 8g; Fat 5g, of which saturates 3g; Cholesterol 29mg; Calcium 9mg; Fibre 0.1g; Sodium 19mg.

Lemon meringue pops

If I had to pick one dish that I remember my mother cooking from my childhood, it is lemon meringue pie, and it is still one of my best-loved desserts today! These little lemon cakes are my take on it – tangy lemon cake, lemon icing and fluffy caramelized meringue. Sunshine baking!

MAKES 20

For the cake
115g/4oz/½ cup butter, softened
115g/4oz/generous ½ cup caster
　(superfine) sugar
2 eggs
115g/4oz/1 cup self-raising
　(self-rising) flour
finely grated rind of 2 lemons
60ml/4 tbsp lemon curd

For the lemon icing
300g/11oz/2¾ cups fondant icing
　(confectioners') sugar
45–60ml/3–4 tbsp lemon juice
a few drops of yellow food
　colouring gel (optional)

For the meringue
60ml/4 tbsp water
200g/7oz/1 cup caster
　(superfine) sugar
5ml/1 tsp vanilla extract
2 egg whites

To serve
20 paper or foil cake cases
20 small wooden skewers

1 Preheat the oven to 180°C/350°F/ Gas 4. Grease and line a 30 x 20cm/ 12 x 8in rectangular cake tin (pan).

2 To make the cake, cream the butter and sugar together until light and fluffy. Beat in the eggs.

3 Sift in the flour and fold into the butter mixture with the lemon rind. Spoon the cake mixture (batter) into the cake tin and level the surface.

4 Bake for 15–20 minutes, or until the cake springs back when pressed and the tip of a sharp knife comes out clean when inserted into the centre. Turn the cake out on to a wire rack to cool.

5 Transfer the cake to a clean work surface or board and cut out 20 small rounds using a 5cm/2in round cutter. Scoop out a small hollow in the top of each mini cake using a melon baller. Spoon the lemon curd into a piping (pastry) bag fitted with a large plain nozzle and pipe a small amount of lemon curd into each hollow.

6 For the icing, put the fondant icing sugar in a bowl with the lemon juice and yellow food colouring gel, if using, and mix to a smooth icing. Place the cakes back on the wire rack with a sheet of foil underneath to catch the icing drips. Spoon the icing over the cakes, covering the sides and tops. Leave until the icing has set.

7 For the meringue, put the water, sugar and vanilla extract in a pan and simmer until the sugar has dissolved. Bring to the boil and boil the syrup until it reaches soft ball stage (114°C/ 238°F on a sugar thermometer).

8 Whisk the egg whites in an electric stand mixer to stiff peaks, then gradually add the hot sugar syrup in a thin drizzle, whisking constantly. Whisk until the meringue mixture cools (about 10–15 minutes). There will be more meringue mixture than you need, but it is difficult to make the meringue in small quantities.

9 Using a separate piping bag fitted with a small star-shaped nozzle, pipe stars of meringue on top of each cake, then use a chef's blowtorch to caramelize the surface of the meringue. Place the cakes into cake cases and insert a wooden skewer into the top of each cake to serve.

Nutritional information: Energy 202kcal/853kJ; Protein 2g; Carbohydrate 39g, of which sugars 33g; Fat 6g, of which saturates 3g; Cholesterol 36mg; Calcium 27mg; Fibre 0.2g; Sodium 75mg.

Tiramisu pops

The name of this Italian dessert can be translated as 'pick me up', which elegantly summarizes the appeal of this dish – strong coffee to wake you up and creamy mascarpone to soothe the soul, all topped with a dusting of cocoa powder. These little pops are perfect with after-dinner coffee.

1 Preheat the oven to 180°C/350°F/ Gas 4. Grease a 24-cup mini muffin tin (pan). For the cakes, cream the butter and sugar together until light and fluffy. Beat in the egg.

2 Sift in the flour and fold in with the dissolved coffee and the sour cream. Divide the cake mixture (batter) among the cups of the mini muffin tin.

3 Bake for 15–20 minutes, until the cakes are golden and spring back when pressed. Transfer to a wire rack to cool.

4 For the cream mousse, allow the melted white chocolate to cool, then place it in a bowl with the mascarpone, crème fraîche and icing sugar, and mix well. Chill for 1 hour or until set.

5 To assemble the cake pops, drizzle a little amaretto liqueur over each cake. Using a piping bag fitted with a small star-shaped nozzle, pipe a star of mousse on to each cake and dust with cocoa powder. Sprinkle with the grated nougat chocolate. When ready to serve, insert a wooden skewer into the base of each pop.

MAKES 24

For the cakes
115g/4oz/½ cup butter, softened
115g/4oz/generous ½ cup caster (superfine) sugar
2 eggs
115g/4oz/1 cup self-raising (self-rising) flour
15ml/1 tbsp instant coffee granules or powder dissolved in 15ml/1 tbsp hot water
15ml/1 tbsp sour cream

For the cream mousse
30g/1¼oz white chocolate, melted
100g/3¾oz/scant ½ cup mascarpone
120ml/4fl oz/½ cup crème fraîche
25ml/1½ tbsp icing (confectioners') sugar, sifted

To assemble and serve
60ml/4 tbsp amaretto liqueur
unsweetened cocoa powder, for dusting
25g/1oz nougat chocolate, grated
24 wooden skewers, to serve

Nutritional information: Energy 192kcal/796kJ; Protein 2g; Carbohydrate 14g, of which sugars 10g; Fat 14g, of which saturates 8g; Cholesterol 48mg; Calcium 44mg; Fibre 0.2g; Sodium 100mg.

Caffè latte pops

Like a smooth glass of caffè latte, these pops offer a creamy caffeine hit. Delicious coffee cake coated in white chocolate and topped with a chocolate coffee bean is a must for all coffee lovers! These are ideal to serve at the end of a dinner party.

MAKES 24

For the cake
50g/2oz/¼ cup butter, softened
50g/2oz/¼ cup caster
   (superfine) sugar
1 egg
50g/2oz/½ cup self-raising
   (self-rising) flour
30ml/2 tbsp instant coffee
   granules or powder dissolved
   in 15ml/1 tbsp hot water
50g/2oz white chocolate, melted
60g/2¼oz/generous ¼ cup
   cream cheese
24 wooden skewers

For the decoration
200g/7oz white chocolate, melted
unsweetened cocoa powder,
   for dusting
24 chocolate coffee beans

1 Preheat the oven to 180°C/350°F/ Gas 4. Grease and line a 20cm/8in square cake tin (pan). To make the cake, cream the butter and caster sugar together until light and fluffy. Beat in the egg.

2 Sift in the flour and fold in with half of the dissolved coffee. Spoon the cake mixture (batter) into the cake tin and level the surface.

3 Bake for 15–20 minutes, or until the cake is golden brown, springs back when gently pressed and the tip of a sharp knife comes out clean when inserted into the centre of the cake. Turn the cake out on to a wire rack and leave to cool completely.

4 Process the cake to crumbs in a food processor. Transfer the crumbs to a bowl, and mix in the rest of the dissolved coffee, the melted white chocolate and cream cheese.

5 Shape the mixture into 24 balls, each about 3cm/1¼in in diameter. Place the balls on a tray and chill in the freezer for 30 minutes.

6 Press a stick into each ball. To decorate, dip each ball into the melted white chocolate, coating all over. Press the sticks into a foam block and dust each pop with a little cocoa powder. Top each pop with a chocolate coffee bean. It is best to do this immediately after dipping in the melted chocolate so that it sticks. Chill until ready to serve.

Nutritional information: Energy 56kcal/239kJ; Protein 1g; Carbohydrate 5g, of which sugars 3g; Fat 4g, of which saturates 2g; Cholesterol 17mg; Calcium 18mg; Fibre 0.1g; Sodium 34mg.

Mocha gold leaf pops

These rich mocha chocolate pops, with hints of coffee and toffee, are the perfect truffle delight, enrobed in a chocolate ganache and topped with glinting edible gold leaf. They add a touch of luxury, and the sprinkle of edible glitter on top means these pops will twinkle the night away.

MAKES 30

For the cake
50g/2oz/¼ cup butter, softened
50g/2oz/¼ cup caster
  (superfine) sugar
1 egg
40g/1½oz/⅓ cup self-raising
  (self-rising) flour
15g/½oz unsweetened cocoa powder
15ml/1 tbsp coffee liqueur
15ml/1 tbsp toffee sauce
25g/1oz/2 tbsp butter, softened
60g/2¼oz/generous ¼ cup
  cream cheese
30 lollipop sticks

For the chocolate ganache
200g/7oz dark (bittersweet)
  chocolate, chopped
105ml/7 tbsp double (heavy) cream
25g/1oz/2 tbsp butter, softened

To decorate
edible gold leaf and edible glitter

1 Preheat the oven to 180°C/350°F/ Gas 4. Grease and line a 20cm/8in square cake tin (pan). For the cake, cream the 50g/2oz/¼ cup butter and the sugar together until light and fluffy. Beat in the egg. Sift in the flour and cocoa powder and fold into the butter mixture.

2 Spoon the cake mixture (batter) into the tin and level the surface. Bake for 15–20 minutes, until the cake springs back when pressed and the tip of a sharp knife comes out clean when inserted into the centre. Turn out on to a wire rack to cool.

3 Process the cooled cake to crumbs in a food processor.

4 Transfer the crumbs to a bowl, add the coffee liqueur, toffee sauce, the 25g/1oz/2 tbsp butter and the cream cheese, and mix together. Shape the mixture into 30 balls, each about 2cm/¾in in diameter. Place them on a tray. Chill in the freezer for 30 minutes.

5 For the ganache, place the chocolate, cream and butter in a heatproof bowl set over a pan of simmering water, taking care that the water does not touch the bottom of the bowl. Stir until you have a smooth, glossy sauce.

6 Press a stick into each ball, then dip each ball into the ganache, coating all over. Press the sticks into a foam block. Add a little edible gold leaf to the top of each pop before the ganache sets and sprinkle with edible glitter. Chill until ready to serve.

Nutritional information: Energy 108kcal/448kJ; Protein 1g; Carbohydrate 7g, of which sugars 6g; Fat 9g, of which saturates 5g; Cholesterol 24mg; Calcium 13mg; Fibre 0.1g; Sodium 46mg.

Matcha macadamia pops

A popular and quirky ingredient, matcha green tea powder is often used to flavour ice cream and custards. It has a lightly smoky taste that works really well in these delicate cupcakes. You can vary the amount of matcha powder to alter the strength of the flavour, if you like.

MAKES 24

For the cakes
115g/4oz/½ cup butter, softened
115g/4oz/generous ½ cup caster
    (superfine) sugar
2 eggs
115g/4oz/1 cup self-raising
    (self-rising) flour, sifted
5ml/1 tsp baking powder
15ml/1 tbsp matcha green tea powder
45ml/3 tbsp crème fraîche
50g/2oz/½ cup macadamia nuts,
    finely chopped

For the icing
400g/14oz/3½ cups fondant icing
    (confectioners') sugar
30–45 ml/2–3 tbsp water
5ml/1 tsp matcha green tea powder
a few drops of green food
    colouring gel

For the caramelized macadamias
100g/3¾oz/generous ½ cup caster
    (superfine) sugar
24 thin pointed wooden skewers
24 whole (shelled) macadamia nuts
    (about 50g/2oz/½ cup)

1 Preheat the oven to 180°C/350°F/ Gas 4. Grease a 24-cup mini muffin tin (pan).

2 For the cakes, using an electric hand mixer or whisk, whisk the butter and sugar together until light and creamy. Whisk in the eggs.

3 Sift the flour and baking powder into the bowl and fold into the butter mixture.

4 Mix the matcha green tea powder and crème fraîche together in a small bowl, then fold this into the cake mixture (batter) with the chopped nuts. Place a heaped teaspoon of mixture into each cup of the mini muffin tin.

5 Bake for 12–15 minutes, or until the cakes are golden and spring back when pressed. Transfer to a wire rack to cool.

6 To make the icing, put the fondant icing sugar, water, matcha green tea powder and a few drops of green food colouring gel in a pan and heat gently, stirring. Place a sheet of foil under the wire rack to catch any icing drips. Dip one cake at a time in the pan, coating the top in the icing, then remove and leave on the wire rack to set. Repeat with all the cakes.

7 For the caramelized macadamias, heat the sugar in a pan until melted and golden in colour. Do not stir, but shake the pan from time to time to prevent the sugar burning. While the caramel is cooking, poke a wooden skewer into each of the macadamias. Remove the pan from the heat and wait for the caramel to start to thicken.

8 Coat a nut completely in caramel, then pull from the pan to get a strand of sugar. Hold the nut downwards while it sets. Repeat with the rest of the nuts. If the caramel becomes too thick, return it to the heat for a few seconds.

9 To serve, gently push a nut-topped skewer into the top of each cake, then gently pull the skewer through the cake so that the nut rests on top.

Nutritional information: Energy 168kcal/706kJ; Protein 1g; Carbohydrate 27g, of which sugars 23g; Fat 7g, of which saturates 3g; Cholesterol 32mg; Calcium 25mg; Fibre 0.2g; Sodium 83mg.

Amaretto pops

Chocolate and amaretto is a decadent flavour combination. These truffles are perfect for winter celebrations served with a cup of strong coffee. Enrobed in a white chocolate case and topped with crushed amaretti, these are naughty but nice treats for a special occasion.

4 Take teaspoonfuls of the ganache and shape them into balls in your hands. Place them on to a silicone mat or a chilled plate. Return to the refrigerator and chill for a further 1 hour, or until the truffles are set.

5 Using a dipping fork, dip each truffle into the melted white chocolate, coating all over. Tap on the side of the bowl to remove any excess chocolate, then place on a wire rack to set.

6 Using a fork, drizzle a pattern of white chocolate on the tops, then sprinkle each truffle with crushed amaretti. Chill until set completely.

MAKES 26

120ml/4fl oz/½ cup double (heavy) cream
15ml/1 tbsp amaretto liqueur
30g/1¼oz/2½ tbsp caster (superfine) sugar
200g/7oz plain (semisweet) chocolate, chopped
50g/2oz/¼ cup butter, melted and cooled
200g/7oz white chocolate, melted
20g/¾oz amaretti, crushed
26 wooden skewers, to serve

1 Place the cream, amaretto liqueur and sugar in a pan and simmer over a gentle heat until the sugar has dissolved, stirring occasionally.

2 Remove from the heat, add the plain chocolate and stir until melted. Beat in the melted butter.

3 Pour the mixture into a shallow tray and chill in the refrigerator for 45–60 minutes, by which time the chocolate ganache will be thick and softly set.

7 Carefully remove the truffles from the wire rack using a sharp knife and insert a skewer into the base of each one. Chill until ready to serve.

Nutritional information: Energy 127kcal/528kJ; Protein 1g; Carbohydrate 11g, of which sugars 11g; Fat 9g, of which saturates 5g; Cholesterol 11mg; Calcium 11mg; Fibre 0g; Sodium 22mg.

After-dinner mint ice cream pops

These little pops are perfect to finish off a meal. They are so simple to make and can be prepared ahead, then kept in the freezer until you are ready to serve them. These pops are sure to delight your guests when they bite through the chocolate shell to reveal a mini choc ice.

MAKES 12

175g/6oz mint ice cream, softened
   (not soft scoop)
12 lollipop sticks
100g/3¾oz white chocolate, melted
100g/3¾oz plain (semisweet)
   chocolate, melted
mint leaves, to decorate (optional)

1 Scoop some softened ice cream into each hole of a 24-hole mini hemispherical silicone mould (each hole should be about 3cm/1¼in in diameter). Freeze until very firm.

2 Remove the ice cream from the moulds and sandwich together the halves to make 12 balls. Freeze again.

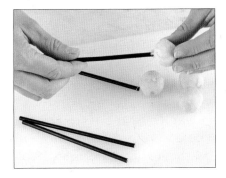

3 Working quickly, and in batches, push a stick into each ball.

4 Quickly dip each ice cream ball into the melted chocolate, coating all over. You should have 6 coated in white chocolate and 6 in plain chocolate.

5 The cold ice cream will set the chocolate very quickly, so if you wish to add a mint leaf to decorate, you should do so immediately, before the chocolate sets too hard. If the chocolate does set too quickly, spoon a little extra melted chocolate over the top of each pop and then quickly add the mint leaf.

6 Return the chocolate pops to the freezer until you are ready to serve.

Nutritional information: Energy 131kcal/548kJ; Protein 2g; Carbohydrate 16g, of which sugars 14g; Fat 7g, of which saturates 4g; Cholesterol 5mg; Calcium 43mg; Fibre 0g; Sodium 21mg.

Mini chocolate Sachertortes

The Hotel Sacher in Vienna is a very special place, said to be the original home of the ultimate Austrian delight, the Sachertorte. It is a rich chocolate and hazelnut cake soaked in apricot glaze and covered in a chocolate ganache. You can pipe an 'S' on the tops, if you want to make them authentic.

MAKES 24

For the cakes
225g/8oz/1 cup butter, softened
225g/8oz/generous 1 cup caster (superfine) sugar
4 eggs
175g/6oz/1½ cups self-raising (self-rising) flour
125g/4¼oz/generous 1 cup ground hazelnuts
100g/3¾oz dark (bittersweet) chocolate, melted
10ml/2 tsp vanilla extract
30ml/2 tbsp apricot jam
30ml/2 tbsp crème fraîche

For the apricot glaze
90ml/6 tbsp apricot jam
juice of 2 lemons

For the ganache
200g/7oz dark (bittersweet) chocolate, chopped
30g/1¼oz/2½ tbsp butter
120ml/4fl oz/½ cup double (heavy) cream

To decorate and serve
chocolate sprinkles
24 paper cake cases, to serve
24 small skewers or forks, to serve

1 Preheat the oven to 180°C/350°F/ Gas 4. Grease and line two 20cm/ 8in square cake tins (pans). For the cakes, cream the butter and sugar until fluffy. Beat in the eggs. Sift in the flour and fold it in with the hazelnuts, chocolate, vanilla extract, jam and crème fraîche.

2 Divide the cake mixture (batter) between the tins and level the surfaces. Bake for 30–35 minutes, until the cakes are firm to the touch and spring back when pressed. Leave the cakes to cool completely in the tins, then turn them out on to a board and cut out 24 rounds using a 5cm/2in round cutter.

3 For the glaze, put the jam and lemon juice in a pan and stir over a gentle heat until melted. Press the mixture through a sieve (strainer). Roll the sides of each cake in the glaze, then dip the top of each cake into the glaze. Transfer to a wire rack and leave to set for 20 minutes.

4 For the ganache, place the chocolate, butter and cream (reserving 15ml/ 1 tbsp cream) in a heatproof bowl set over a pan of simmering water, taking care that the water does not touch the bottom of the bowl. Stir until you have a smooth, glossy sauce. Remove from the heat and leave to cool slightly, then stir in the reserved cream. Leave the ganache until it starts to thicken.

5 Spread the ganache around the edges of each cake, then return them to the wire rack. Place a spoonful of ganache on top of each cake and smooth out.

6 Decorate with sprinkles. Once the ganache and chocolate are set, place each cake in a paper cake case and insert a small skewer or fork into the top of each cake.

Nutritional information: Energy 221kcal/923kJ; Protein 3g; Carbohydrate 22g, of which sugars 17g; Fat 14g, of which saturates 6g; Cholesterol 60mg; Calcium 44mg; Fibre 0.8g; Sodium 101mg.

Triple chocolate brownie pops

Rich, indulgent brownie pops are perfect for any occasion – dipped in melted white chocolate and decorated with brightly coloured sugar sprinkles, these are a chocolate lover's dream! You could add a handful of chopped nuts of your choice to the recipe for equally delicious results.

MAKES 24

For the brownies
250g/9oz/generous 1 cup butter
350g/12oz plain (semisweet)
   chocolate, roughly chopped
250g/9oz/scant 1⅓ cups caster
   (superfine) sugar
250g/9oz/generous 1 cup soft dark
   brown sugar
5 eggs
5ml/1 tsp vanilla extract
200g/7oz/1¼ cups plain
   (all-purpose) flour, sifted
200g/7oz white chocolate chips

To decorate and serve
24 lollipop sticks
150g/5oz white chocolate, melted
coloured sugar sprinkles and
   chocolate sprinkles

1 Preheat the oven to 180°C/350°F/ Gas 4. Grease and line a 30 x 20cm/ 12 x 8in deep baking tin (pan).

2 For the brownies, put the butter and plain chocolate in a heatproof bowl set over a pan of simmering water, taking care that the bottom of the bowl does not touch the water. Stir until melted and combined. Remove from the heat and leave to cool.

3 Using an electric hand mixer or whisk, whisk the caster sugar, brown sugar, eggs and vanilla extract in a large bowl until the mixture is very light and has doubled in volume. While you continue to whisk, slowly pour in the cooled melted chocolate mixture, whisking until fully incorporated.

4 Sift in the flour and fold into the chocolate mixture with the chocolate chips. Pour the brownie mixture (batter) into the tin.

5 Bake for 25–35 minutes, or until it has formed a crust and the tip of a sharp knife inserted into the centre comes out clean. Leave the brownie to cool completely in the tin. Once cool, turn out on to a clean work surface or board.

6 Cut out 24 rounds of brownie using a 5cm/2in round cutter.

7 Insert a stick into each brownie. To decorate, dip each brownie pop into the melted white chocolate, then decorate with sprinkles and leave to set before serving.

Nutritional information: Energy 295kcal/1235kJ; Protein 4g; Carbohydrate 33g, of which sugars 26g; Fat 17g, of which saturates 10g; Cholesterol 72mg; Calcium 65mg; Fibre 0.3g; Sodium 58mg.

Chocolate mud pie pops

These little pops are inspired by the classic chocolate dessert, Mississippi Mud Pie – chocolate sponge, chocolate ganache and chocolate mousse. This recipe contains no fewer than 6 different types of chocolate, including the cocoa powder and chocolate curls – a true chocoholic's delight!

3 Bake for 15–20 minutes, or until the cake springs back when pressed and the tip of a sharp knife comes out clean when inserted into the centre. Turn the cake out on to a wire rack to cool.

4 Process the cake to crumbs in a food processor. Transfer the cake crumbs to a bowl, add the cream cheese and melted chocolate and mix together.

5 Shape the mixture into 28 even-sized balls, place them on a tray and chill in the freezer for 30 minutes.

6 Meanwhile, prepare the chocolate mousse. Whip the cream to stiff peaks. Allow the melted chocolates to cool, then fold them in until you have a smooth mousse. Chill for 1 hour.

7 Press a stick into each ball. For the coating, dip half of the balls into the melted white chocolate and half into the plain chocolate. Press the sticks into a foam block and leave to set, then chill until ready to serve.

8 To serve, using a piping (pastry) bag fitted with a large star-shaped nozzle, pipe a star of mousse on to each pop. Top with chocolate curls.

MAKES 28

For the cake
50g/2oz/¼ cup butter, softened
50g/2oz/¼ cup caster (superfine) sugar
1 egg
50g/2oz/½ cup self-raising (self-rising) flour
15ml/1 tbsp unsweetened cocoa powder
100g/3¾oz/scant ½ cup cream cheese
100g/3¾oz milk chocolate, melted
28 lollipop sticks

For the chocolate coating
100g/3¾oz white chocolate, melted
100g/3¾oz plain (semisweet) chocolate, melted

For the chocolate mousse
200ml/7fl oz/scant 1 cup double (heavy) cream
50g/2oz nougat chocolate, melted
50g/2oz milk chocolate, melted

For the decoration
chocolate caramel curls

1 Preheat the oven to 180°C/350°F/ Gas 4. Grease and line a 20cm/8in square cake tin (pan).

2 For the cake, cream the butter and sugar together until light and fluffy. Beat in the egg. Sift in the flour and cocoa powder, then fold in with a spatula. Spoon the mixture into the cake tin and level the surface.

Nutritional information: Energy 102kcal/424 kJ; Protein 1g; Carbohydrate 10g, of which sugars 8g; Fat 7g, of which saturates 4g; Cholesterol 17mg; Calcium 31mg; Fibre 0.1g; Sodium 41mg.

Chocolate chilli pops

Chilli may seem a strange accompaniment to chocolate, but it really does enhance the flavour of the cocoa powder. Bars of chilli-flavoured chocolate are available in most supermarkets. If you can find red lollipop sticks that are suitable for food use, they will display these fiery pops wonderfully.

MAKES 40

For the cakes
50g/2oz/¼ cup butter, softened
50g/2oz/¼ cup caster
  (superfine) sugar
1 egg
40g/1½oz/⅓ cup self-raising
  (self-rising) flour
25g/1oz unsweetened cocoa powder
30ml/2 tbsp sour cream
40g/1½oz plain (semisweet) chilli
  chocolate, finely grated
40 lollipop sticks

For the decoration
75g/3oz plain (semisweet) chilli
  chocolate, melted
red heart sprinkles

1 Preheat the oven to 180°C/350°F/Gas 4. Grease two 20-hole mini hemispherical silicone moulds.

2 To make the cakes, cream the butter and sugar together until light and fluffy. Beat in the egg.

3 Sift in the flour and cocoa powder and fold in with the sour cream and grated chocolate. Spoon the cake mixture (batter) into the holes of the prepared moulds, dividing it evenly.

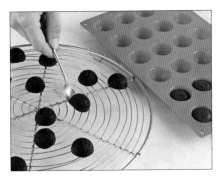

4 Bake the cakes for 10–15 minutes, or until the cakes spring back when gently pressed. Transfer to a wire rack to cool. Once cool, poke a stick into the base of each cake.

5 Press the sticks into a foam block. To decorate, drizzle the pops with melted chilli chocolate and sprinkle with red heart sprinkles. Let the chocolate set before serving.

COOK'S TIP
If you can't find chilli chocolate, you can use plain (semisweet) chocolate and add a pinch of hot chilli powder to the cake mixture instead.

Nutritional information: Energy 35kcal/144kJ; Protein 0g; Carbohydrate 3g, of which sugars 3g; Fat 2g, of which saturates 1g; Cholesterol 9mg; Calcium 4mg; Fibre 0g; Sodium 16mg.

Churros with hot chocolate sauce

These crispy fried churros (Spanish doughnuts) are a delicious treat, served with a thick, hot chocolate sauce to dip them into. Turning the churros into pops by inserting wooden skewers means that your fingers will remain sugar- and chocolate-free.

MAKES 30

For the churros
125g/4¼oz/generous 1 cup plain (all-purpose) flour
250ml/8fl oz/1 cup water
100g/3¾oz/scant ½ cup butter
5ml/1 tsp vanilla extract
3 eggs, beaten
sunflower oil, for frying
45ml/3 tbsp caster (superfine) sugar
5ml/1 tsp ground cinnamon
30 wooden skewers

For the hot chocolate sauce
120ml/4fl oz/½ cup full-fat (whole) milk
120ml/4fl oz/½ cup double (heavy) cream
100g/3¾oz dark (bittersweet) chocolate, chopped
1 cinnamon stick

1 To make the churros, sift the flour twice into a bowl to remove lumps and to add as much air as possible.

2 Place the water, butter and vanilla extract in a pan. Heat gently until the butter has melted. Bring to the boil, then quickly add all the flour in one go and beat hard using a wooden spoon until a ball of dough forms.

3 Remove the pan from the heat and leave to cool for 10 minutes. Beat in the eggs, a little at a time, beating well between each addition. Spoon the mixture into a piping (pastry) bag fitted with a star-shaped nozzle.

4 Pour sunflower oil into a large, heavy pan to a depth of 7.5–10cm/3–4in.

5 Heat the oil until a small piece of bread, added to the oil, immediately sizzles and turns golden brown.

6 Carefully pipe the churros mixture directly into the hot oil in lengths of about 10cm/4in, holding the piping bag in one hand and scissors in the other. Use the scissors to cut the dough at the desired length. Cook the churros, five at a time, for 3–5 minutes, then turn over and cook until golden brown all over. Remove each batch of churros using a slotted spoon and drain on kitchen paper.

7 Mix the caster sugar and ground cinnamon together on a plate.

8 Toss the warm churros in the sugar mixture, then insert a skewer into each one.

9 To make the hot chocolate sauce, put the milk, cream, chocolate and cinnamon stick in a pan and heat over a gentle heat until the chocolate has melted and the sauce is smooth and combined, stirring occasionally. Remove and discard the cinnamon stick. Serve the hot chocolate sauce with the warm churros.

Nutritional information: Energy 123kcal/512kJ; Protein 2g; Carbohydrate 7g, of which sugars 4g; Fat 10g, of which saturates 4g; Cholesterol 37mg; Calcium 19mg; Fibre 0.2g; Sodium 32mg.

Chocolate mocha fondue sticks

Not a pop as such, but no book of sweet treats on sticks could be complete without this 1980s dinner-party favourite. You could serve it in a fondue pot in the centre of the table, or, as here, in warmed individual coffee cups. It will remain melted for about 30 minutes.

SERVES 8

For the fondue
250g/9oz plain (semisweet)
   chocolate, chopped
100g/3¾oz white chocolate,
   chopped
60ml/4 tbsp Tia Maria or other
   coffee liqueur
150ml/¼ pint/⅔ cup double
   (heavy) cream, plus extra
   for decoration

For dipping
wooden skewers or dipping forks
strawberries, seedless grapes,
   amaretti, sponge fingers or plain
   sponge cake and marshmallows

COOK'S TIP
If the fondue starts to get too firm, simply put it back over the pan and heat until melted.

1 Place the plain and white chocolate in a heatproof bowl set over a pan of simmering water. Add the Tia Maria and cream. Stir until the chocolate has melted and you have a smooth sauce.

2 Insert wooden skewers or dipping forks into the dipping ingredients, or give each diner a skewer or fork and place the ingredients for dipping on serving plates.

3 Transfer the sauce to warmed cups. Drizzle a little extra cream over the top and swirl with a cocktail stick (toothpick) to make a pretty pattern. Serve with the dipping ingredients.

Nutritional information: Energy 338kcal/1407kJ; Protein 3g; Carbohydrate 30g, of which sugars 30g; Fat 23g, of which saturates 14g; Cholesterol 28mg; Calcium 53mg; Fibre 0g; Sodium 20mg.

Holiday and special occasion pops

Some events call for something memorable, and this chapter is full of ideas to make innovative baked treats for birthdays, weddings and other special occasions. Surprise your mother on Mother's Day with a homemade bouquet of flowers – a lovingly crafted set of flower-shaped cookie pops, beautifully decorated and displayed in a bunch. There are also plenty of festive pops to get you and your family in the mood for Christmas, such as Gingerbread House Pops, delicate meringue Snowmen Pops and glittery Christmas Tree Pops.

Birthday cake pops

These charming little cakes, holding mini candles, make an unusual centrepiece for a birthday celebration. Topped with purple icing, vanilla buttercream and sprinkles, they look almost too pretty to eat. You can also add extra party decorations, if you like.

MAKES 10

For the cakes
50g/2oz/¼ cup butter, softened
50g/2oz/¼ cup caster
  (superfine) sugar
1 egg
50g/2oz/½ cup self-raising
  (self-rising) flour
5ml/1 tsp vanilla extract
15ml/1 tbsp sour cream

For the fondant icing
200g/7oz/1¾ cups fondant icing
  (confectioners') sugar, sifted
45–60ml/3–4 tbsp water
a few drops of purple food
  colouring gel

For the buttercream icing
90g/3½oz/¾ cup icing
  (confectioners') sugar, sifted
30g/1¼oz/2½ tbsp butter, softened
15ml/1 tbsp milk

To decorate and serve
coloured sugar sprinkles
10 mini candles, cut to 1cm/½in,
  and candle holders
10 wooden skewers
10 mini marshmallows

1 Preheat the oven to 180°C/350°F/ Gas 4. Grease a 10-cup straight-sided mini muffin tin (pan). For the cakes, cream the butter and caster sugar together until fluffy. Beat in the egg.

2 Sift in the flour and fold in with the vanilla extract and sour cream using a spatula. Divide the mixture between the cups of the prepared tin.

3 Bake for 12–15 minutes, or until the cakes are golden brown and spring back when gently pressed. Transfer to a wire rack to cool.

4 For the fondant icing, put the fondant icing sugar and water in a bowl with the purple food colouring gel and whisk to a smooth thin icing. Place a sheet of foil underneath the wire rack. Dip each cake into the icing so that it is completely coated. Return to the wire rack and leave to set.

5 For the buttercream, sift the icing sugar into a bowl, add the butter and half of the milk. Whisk for 3 minutes, until creamy; add more milk if needed.

6 Using a piping (pastry) bag fitted with a small star-shaped nozzle, pipe a ring of stars around the top of each cake. Decorate with sugar sprinkles. Add a mini candle to the top of each cake in a candle holder. To serve, insert a skewer into the base of each cake, securing with a mini marshmallow.

Nutritional information: Energy 223kcal/940kJ; Protein 1g; Carbohydrate 40g, of which sugars 36g; Fat 8g, of which saturates 5g; Cholesterol 41mg; Calcium 22mg; Fibre 0.2g; Sodium 80mg.

Wedding cake pops

These delicate mini tiered wedding cakes make perfect favours at a wedding. The rich vanilla sponge truffles, coated in white chocolate and decorated to look like a replica of a full-sized wedding cake, would delight any bride. Change the icing colour to fit in with the colour scheme of your wedding.

MAKES 16

For the cakes
95g/3¾oz/scant ½ cup butter, softened
50g/2oz/¼ cup caster
   (superfine) sugar
1 egg
50g/2oz/½ cup self-raising
   (self-rising) flour
10ml/2 tsp vanilla extract
90g/3½oz/scant ½ cup cream cheese
16 wooden skewers

**For the decoration and buttercream
   icing**
200g/7oz white chocolate, melted
100g/3¾oz/scant 1 cup icing
   (confectioners') sugar
30g/1¼oz/2½ tbsp butter, softened
about 15ml/1 tbsp milk
a few drops of pink food colouring gel
16 sugar flowers and edible glitter,
   to decorate

1 Preheat the oven to 180°C/350°F/ Gas 4. Grease and line a 20cm/8in square cake tin (pan).

2 For the cakes, cream 50g/2oz/ ¼ cup butter and the sugar together until light and fluffy. Beat in the egg. Sift in the flour and fold in with 5ml/1 tsp vanilla extract. Spoon the cake mixture (batter) into the cake tin and level the surface.

3 Bake for 15–20 minutes, until the cake is golden and the tip of a sharp knife comes out clean when inserted into the centre. Leave to cool in the tin for a couple of minutes, then turn out on to a wire rack to cool completely.

4 Process the cake to crumbs in a food processor. Transfer the crumbs to a bowl, add the remaining butter, the cream cheese and the rest of the vanilla extract. Mix together.

5 Shape the mixture to make sixteen 4cm/1½in cylindrical discs, sixteen 2.5cm/1in discs and sixteen 1cm/½in discs. Stack one of each disc in towers to create 16 mini three-tiered wedding cakes. Place them on a tray and chill in the freezer for 30 minutes.

6 Remove the mini wedding cakes from the freezer and press a wooden skewer into the base of each one. To decorate, dip each tier into the melted white chocolate, coating all over. Press the wooden skewers into a foam block and leave to set.

7 To prepare the buttercream icing, sift the icing sugar into a large bowl and add the butter and milk. Whisk together for about 3 minutes, or until light and creamy, adding a little more milk if the icing is too stiff. Stir in the pink food colouring.

8 Using a piping (pastry) bag fitted with a small star-shaped nozzle, pipe small stars of buttercream around each tier. Top each mini wedding cake with a sugar flower, fixing with melted chocolate, and sprinkle with edible glitter. Chill until ready to serve.

Nutritional information: Energy 213kcal/891kJ; Protein 2g; Carbohydrate 22g, of which sugars 20g; Fat 13g, of which saturates 8g; Cholesterol 37mg; Calcium 56mg; Fibre 0.1g; Sodium 96mg.

Valentine pops

If you want to treat a loved one on Valentine's Day, bake them some of these homemade cookie pops – flavoured with roses, the flower of love. These colourful cookies are decorated with sugar hearts and pretty pink icing, and you can colour the stick red with food colouring for extra effect.

3 Cut out 8 heart shapes using a 10cm/4in heart-shaped cutter. Place the cookies on the prepared baking sheets and insert an ice lolly stick into the base of each cookie, ensuring that the top of the stick is completely covered in cookie dough.

4 Bake for 10–15 minutes, or until golden brown. Leave the cookies to cool completely on the baking sheets.

5 To make the icing, sift the icing sugar into a bowl and stir in enough warm water to give a smooth, thick icing. Stir in a few drops of pink food colouring gel.

6 Spread the icing evenly over the cookies and decorate with the sugar heart sprinkles. Leave the icing to set before serving.

MAKES 8

For the cookies
50g/2oz/¼ cup caster (superfine) sugar
115g/4oz/½ cup butter, softened
175g/6oz/1½ cups plain (all-purpose) flour, plus extra for dusting
15ml/1 tbsp rose syrup
15ml/1 tbsp milk (optional)
8 ice lolly (popsicle) sticks

For the icing and decoration
200g/7oz/1¾ cups icing (confectioners') sugar
45–60ml/3–4 tbsp warm water
a few drops of pink food colouring gel
sugar heart sprinkles, to decorate

1 For the cookies, using an electric hand mixer or whisk, whisk the sugar and butter until pale and creamy. Sift in the flour, add the rose syrup and mix together to form a soft dough. If the mixture is too dry, add the milk, mixing well. Wrap the dough in clear film (plastic wrap) and chill for 1 hour.

2 Preheat the oven to 180°C/350°F/ Gas 4. Grease and line two baking sheets. On a floured surface, roll out the dough to a thickness of 8mm/⅜in.

COOK'S TIP
These cookies look very pretty presented in cellophane bags, tied with ribbons to decorate.

Nutritional information: Energy 310kcal/1305kJ; Protein 2g; Carbohydrate 51g, of which sugars 34g; Fat 12g, of which saturates 8g; Cholesterol 31mg; Calcium 37mg; Fibre 0.8g; Sodium 97mg.

Mother's Day cookie flowers

Mothers do so much for us, and on Mother's Day it is important to show them that we care.
I find that a home baked gift is more special and these cookies are sure to impress when wrapped
up in cellophane and tied with a large ribbon bow. Arrange them on a sheet of stiff card, for stability.

MAKES ABOUT 20

For the cookies
50g/2oz/¼ cup caster
　(superfine) sugar
115g/4oz/½ cup butter, softened
175g/6oz/1½ cups self-raising
　(self-rising) flour, plus extra
　for dusting
finely grated rind of 1 orange and
　1 lemon
15ml/1 tbsp milk (optional)
20 thin wooden skewers

For the glacé icing
200g/7oz/1¾ cups icing
　(confectioners') sugar, sifted
45–60ml/3–4 tbsp warm water

**For the buttercream icing and
　decoration**
225g/8oz/2 cups icing
　(confectioners') sugar, sifted
40g/1½oz/3 tbsp butter, softened
15–30ml/1–2 tbsp milk
a few drops of food colouring
　gel(s) of your choice
100g/3¾oz white chocolate, melted
jelly sweets (candies), to decorate

1 For the cookies, using an electric
hand mixer, whisk the sugar and
butter together until pale and creamy.
Sift in the flour, add the citrus rinds
and mix to form a soft dough. If the
mixture is too dry, add the milk,
mixing well. Wrap the dough in clear
film (plastic wrap). Chill for 1 hour.

2 Meanwhile, preheat the oven to
180°C/350°F/Gas 4. Grease and line
two baking sheets.

3 On a lightly floured surface, roll out
the dough to 8mm/⅜in thickness and
cut out a variety of about 20 different-
sized flower shapes using cutters.

4 Place the cookies on the baking
sheets and insert a skewer into each
one, ensuring that the top of the
skewer is completely covered in
dough. Bake for 10–15 minutes, until
golden. Leave the cookies to cool
completely on the baking sheets.
Meanwhile, for the glacé icing, mix
the icing sugar with enough warm
water to make a smooth, thick icing.

5 Place one-third of the cookies on a
wire rack with a sheet of foil
underneath. Spread the glacé icing
evenly over the cookies. Place a sweet
in the centre of each and leave to set.

6 For the buttercream icing, whisk the
icing sugar, butter and milk until light
and creamy. Divide the buttercream
between several bowls and colour each
with a different food colouring gel.
Spoon each buttercream into a separate
piping (pastry) bag, fitted with a rose-
or chrysanthemum-effect nozzle. Pipe
petals on to half of the un-iced cookies.

7 To decorate the remaining un-iced
cookies, colour the white chocolate
with food colouring gels and spread
evenly over the cookies. Add a sweet
to the centre. When the icing and
chocolate on all the cookies has set,
assemble them in an arrangement and
wrap up into a bouquet in clear
cellophane. Tie with a ribbon bow.

Nutritional information: Energy 142kcal/595kJ; Protein 1g; Carbohydrate 21g, of which sugars 14g; Fat 7g, of which saturates 4g; Cholesterol 17mg; Calcium 35mg; Fibre 0.4g; Sodium 81mg.

Chocolate Easter egg pops

These little chocolate eggs are a delightful Easter celebration – there is nothing more creative and rewarding than making your own Easter eggs! You need small plastic Easter egg moulds to make these pops. They are available from good cookshops and online.

MAKES 8

For the eggs
200g/7oz milk or plain (semisweet)
  chocolate, melted
250g/9oz/2¼ cups royal icing
  (confectioners') sugar, sifted
45ml/3 tbsp water
a few drops of pink and yellow
  food colouring gels

To decorate and serve
8 sugar flowers
8 thin wooden skewers

COOK'S TIP
Adjust the amount of chocolate for different-sized moulds. This recipe is for moulds 6cm/2½in in height and 3cm/1¼in in width.

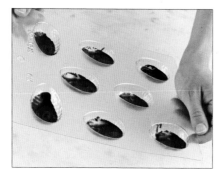

1 Pour the melted chocolate into Easter egg moulds and spread out so that each mould is coated in chocolate. Leave to set for about 15 minutes, then apply a second coat of chocolate to each egg mould. Chill until set.

2 Put the royal icing sugar and water in a bowl and whisk together for about 5 minutes, or until the icing is light and airy, and holds its shape when you lift the whisk up.

3 Add a few drops of pink food colouring gel and beat again.

4 Remove the chocolate moulds from the refrigerator and carefully pop the chocolate egg shells out. Trim the edges of each eggshell using a sharp knife. Touch the chocolate as little as possible to avoid making fingerprints.

5 Hold two half shells together and, using a piping (pastry) bag fitted with a small star-shaped nozzle, pipe stars of icing over the join all around the egg. Pipe a small star of icing on the front of the egg and top with a sugar flower. Return to the refrigerator and repeat with all the remaining egg shells.

6 When ready to serve, carefully push a wooden skewer into the base of each egg.

Nutritional information: Energy 250kcal/1059 kJ; Protein 1g; Carbohydrate 49g, of which sugars 48g; Fat 7g, of which saturates 4g; Cholesterol 2mg; Calcium 9mg; Fibre 0g; Sodium 5mg.

Easter cookie pops

If chocolate is not your favourite thing at Easter, why not try these delicious Easter treats? Scented with the classic Simnel cake spices – cinnamon and nutmeg – they are decorated with pretty pastel icings, and tied with matching ribbon bows. These would make a charming Easter gift.

MAKES 14

For the cookies
50g/2oz/¼ cup caster
   (superfine) sugar
115g/4oz/½ cup butter, softened
175g/6oz/1½ cups self-raising
   (self-rising) flour, plus extra
   for dusting
5ml/1 tsp ground cinnamon
5ml/1 tsp mixed spice
   (apple pie spice)
1.5ml/¼ tsp freshly grated nutmeg
15ml/1 tbsp milk (optional)
14 thin wooden skewers

For the icing
200g/7oz/1¾ cups icing
   (confectioners') sugar
30–45ml/2–3 tbsp warm water
a few drops of pink, blue, yellow
   and green food colouring gels

To decorate
thin ribbons

1 To make the cookies, using an electric hand mixer or whisk, whisk the caster sugar and butter together until pale and creamy. Sift the flour into the bowl, add the spices and mix together to form a soft dough. If the mixture is too dry, add the milk, mixing well. Wrap the dough in clear film (plastic wrap) and chill in the refrigerator for 1 hour.

2 Preheat the oven to 180°C/350°F/ Gas 4. Grease and line two baking sheets. On a lightly floured surface, roll out the cookie dough to 8mm/⅜in thickness.

3 Cut out 14 Easter egg shapes using an 8 x 6cm/3¼ x 2½in oval cutter, re-rolling the dough as necessary.

4 Place the cookies on the prepared baking sheets and insert a wooden skewer into the base of each cookie, ensuring that the top of the skewer is completely covered in cookie dough.

5 Bake for 12–15 minutes, or until golden. Leave the cookies to cool completely on the baking sheets.

6 To make the icing, sift the icing sugar into a bowl and stir in enough warm water to give a smooth, thick icing. Divide the icing between four bowls and colour each portion a different colour by stirring in a few drops of food colouring gel.

7 Using piping (pastry) bags fitted with small plain nozzles, pipe decorative icing in pink, blue, yellow and green on each cookie. Leave the icing to set, then tie thin ribbons in bows on each wooden skewer before serving.

Nutritional information: Energy 173kcal/730kJ; Protein 1g; Carbohydrate 28g, of which sugars 19g; Fat 7g, of which saturates 4g; Cholesterol 18mg; Calcium 9mg; Fibre 0.5g; Sodium 97mg.

4th July pops

When celebrating this American holiday, why not make some of these cute red, white and blue pops, decorated with patriotic sugar stars? They could also be modified to become Union Jack pops! You can also change the colours of the layers of sponge to make them suitable for other occasions.

3 Bake for 15–20 minutes, until the cakes are firm to the touch and spring back when pressed in the centre. Turn out on to a wire rack to cool.

4 For the buttercream icing, sift the icing sugar into a bowl, add the butter and half of the buttermilk. Whisk for 3 minutes, or until light and creamy, adding more buttermilk if necessary.

5 Place the blue cake on a cutting board and cover the top with a thin layer of buttercream. Place the white cake on top and again cover the top with a thin layer of buttercream. Top with the red cake and cover this with a thicker layer of buttercream, reserving a little for decoration. Chill the cake until the buttercream has set.

6 Trim away the edges of the cake to make a neat square. Cut the cake into 25 small squares, wiping the knife clean between each cut. Using a piping (pastry) bag fitted with a star-shaped nozzle, pipe a star of the reserved icing on each cake. Decorate with sugar stars. When ready to serve, insert a stick into the base of each cake, securing with a mini marshmallow, if necessary.

MAKES 25

For the layer cakes
115g/4oz/½ cup butter, softened
115g/4oz/generous ½ cup caster (superfine) sugar
2 eggs
115g/4oz/1 cup self-raising (self-rising) flour
30ml/2 tbsp natural (plain) yogurt
a few drops of red food colouring gel
a few drops of blue food colouring gel

For the buttercream icing
260g/9½oz/2⅓ cups icing (confectioners') sugar, sifted
50g/2oz/¼ cup butter, softened
15–30ml/1–2 tbsp buttermilk

To decorate and serve
red, white and blue sugar stars
25 lollipop sticks
25 mini marshmallows (optional)

1 Preheat the oven to 180°C/350°F/ Gas 4. Grease and line three 20cm/8in square cake tins (pans). For the cakes, cream the butter and sugar together until light and fluffy. Beat in the eggs.

2 Sift in the flour and fold in with the yogurt. Divide the mixture among three bowls. Add the red food colouring to one and the blue to another. Leave the third bowl plain. Spoon each mixture (batter) into one of the cake tins and level the surfaces.

Nutritional information: Energy 131kcal/551kJ; Protein 1g; Carbohydrate 19g, of which sugars 6g; Fat 6g, of which saturates 4g; Cholesterol 33mg; Calcium 23mg; Fibre 0.2g; Sodium 66mg.

Halloween ghost pops

When little ghosts and ghouls come calling on All Hallows' Eve, greet them with Halloween ghost pops to put in their goody bags. To display them, why not hollow out a small pumpkin and fill with a foam block, covered with foil? Poke the sticks in and then cover the foil with mini marshmallows.

MAKES 24

For the cakes
50g/2oz/¼ cup butter, softened
50g/2oz/¼ cup caster
    (superfine) sugar
1 egg
50g/2oz/½ cup self-raising
    (self-rising) flour
15ml/1 tbsp natural (plain) yogurt

**For the buttercream icing and
    decoration**
200g/7oz/1¾ cups icing
    (confectioners') sugar,
    plus extra for dusting
40g/1½oz/3 tbsp butter, softened
30ml/2 tbsp milk
a few drops of black food
    colouring gel
300g/11oz ready-to-roll white
    icing (sugarpaste)

To serve
24 lollipop sticks
24 mini marshmallows

1 Preheat the oven to 180°C/350°F/
Gas 4. Grease a 24-cup mini muffin
tin (pan).

2 For the cakes, cream the butter and
sugar together until light and fluffy.
Beat in the egg. Sift in the flour and
fold it in with the yogurt. Spoon a
heaped teaspoon of cake mixture
(batter) into each cup of the prepared
mini muffin tin.

3 Bake for 12–15 minutes, until the
cakes are golden and spring back when
pressed. Transfer to a wire rack to cool.

4 To prepare the buttercream icing,
sift the icing sugar into a bowl, add
the butter and half of the milk.
Whisk together for about 3 minutes,
or until light and creamy, adding
a little more milk if necessary.
Reserve a heaped tablespoonful of
the buttercream and colour this with
a few drops of black food colouring
gel. Set this aside for decoration.

5 Invert the cakes so that the smaller
base of each is facing upwards.
Using a round-bladed knife, cover
the sides and top of each cake with
white buttercream icing.

6 Roll out the ready-to-roll icing on
an icing sugar-dusted surface until it
is very thin.

7 Using an 8cm/3¼in round cutter,
cut out 24 rounds of icing. Drape
one over each cake, inserting a stick
into the base of each. Secure the base
with a mini marshmallow.

8 Using a piping (pastry) bag fitted
with a very small plain nozzle, pipe
two small black dots for eyes on each
ghost, using the reserved black icing.

Nutritional information: Energy 126kcal/532 kJ; Protein 1g; Carbohydrate 25g, of which sugars 23g; Fat 3g, of which saturates 2g; Cholesterol 18mg; Calcium 13mg; Fibre 0.1g; Sodium 40mg.

Pumpkin pops

These splendid little pumpkin cakes are ideal to serve at a Halloween party. Deliciously flavoured with pumpkin and cinnamon, and intricately decorated as mini pumpkins with chocolate stems and green leaves, these cake pops look almost too good to eat.

MAKES 30

For the pumpkin cake
50g/2oz/¼ cup butter, softened
50g/2oz/¼ cup soft light brown sugar
1 egg
50g/2oz/½ cup self-raising (self-rising) flour
45ml/3 tbsp pumpkin purée
10ml/2 tsp ground cinnamon
5ml/1 tsp vanilla extract
15ml/1 tbsp maple syrup
100g/3¾oz white chocolate, melted
75g/3oz/scant ⅓ cup cream cheese

For the decoration
300g/10½oz white chocolate, melted
a few drops of orange food colouring gel
30 lollipop sticks
orange chocolate sticks, cut into 30 pieces, 1cm/½in long

For the buttercream icing
50g/2oz/½ cup icing (confectioners') sugar
25g/1oz/2 tbsp butter, softened
5ml/1 tsp milk
a few drops of green food colouring gel

1 Preheat the oven to 180°C/350°F/Gas 4. Grease and line a 20cm/8in square cake tin (pan). For the cake, cream the butter and sugar together until light and fluffy. Beat in the egg.

2 Sift in the flour and fold in with the pumpkin purée, cinnamon, vanilla extract and maple syrup. Spoon the mixture (batter) into the cake tin. Level the surface. Bake for 15–20 minutes, until the tip of a sharp knife comes out clean when inserted into the centre. Turn out on to a wire rack to cool.

3 Process the cake to crumbs in a food processor. Transfer the crumbs to a bowl, add the melted white chocolate and cream cheese, and mix together.

4 Shape the mixture into 30 balls, then squash each one between your fingertips to make a slightly flattened ball. Using a cocktail stick (toothpick), make five indentations around the edges of the ball so that you have small pumpkin shapes. Place on a tray and chill in the freezer for 30 minutes.

5 For the decoration, colour the white chocolate by stirring in the orange food colouring gel. Press a stick into the base of each pumpkin. Dip in the melted orange-coloured chocolate, coating all over. Insert an orange chocolate stick 'stalk' into the centre of each pumpkin. Press the sticks into a foam block and leave to set.

6 To prepare the buttercream icing, sift the icing sugar into a bowl, add the butter, milk and a few drops of green food colouring gel and whisk until light and creamy but fairly stiff.

7 Spoon the buttercream into a piping (pastry) bag fitted with a leaf-shaped nozzle and pipe 2 leaves on to each pumpkin either side of the chocolate stick stalk. Change to a very small plain nozzle and pipe thin swirls of icing on to each pumpkin to represent the pumpkin fronds. Chill the pumpkin pops until you are ready to serve them.

Nutritional information: Energy 110kcal/461kJ; Protein 2g; Carbohydrate 11g, of which sugars 10g; Fat 7g, of which saturates 4g; Cholesterol 14mg; Calcium 49mg; Fibre 0.1g; Sodium 42mg.

Thanksgiving pecan and pumpkin pie pops

These little puffed pumpkin pies, bursting with sweet buttery pumpkin purée, nuts and spices, are a perfect snack for Thanksgiving or Halloween. You can make the pops into any shape you like. I have used a pumpkin cutter but you could make stars or circle pops, if you prefer.

MAKES 10

50g/2oz/½ cup pecans
30g/1¼oz/scant ¼ cup cream cheese
30ml/2 tbsp pumpkin purée
5ml/1 tsp ground cinnamon
20g/¾oz/1½ tbsp caster
  (superfine) sugar
plain (all-purpose) flour, for dusting
375g/13oz ready-made puff pastry
10 ice lolly (popsicle) sticks
beaten egg, for brushing
sugar sprinkles, pumpkin seeds
  or cinnamon sugar, to decorate

1 Preheat the oven to 180°C/350°F/ Gas 4. Grease and line two baking sheets. Blitz the pecans in a food processor until finely chopped. Add the cream cheese, pumpkin purée, cinnamon and caster sugar to the food processor and blitz to a purée.

2 On a lightly floured surface, roll out the puff pastry to 3mm/⅛in thickness. Using a pumpkin-shaped cutter, cut out 20 pumpkin shapes. Arrange 10 of them on the baking sheets. Place a small mound of pumpkin mixture in the centre of the 10 pastry shapes. Wet the edges of the pastry with water and top with a second pumpkin shape.

3 Insert an ice lolly stick between the pastry layers into the pumpkin purée of each pie. Press the pastry edges together, sealing by pressing down with the prongs of a fork. It is important to seal the pastry around the ice lolly sticks tightly so that the filling does not leak out.

4 Brush the tops with the beaten egg, then sprinkle with sugar sprinkles, pumpkin seeds or cinnamon sugar.

5 Bake for 10–15 minutes, or until the pastry is golden. Leave to cool slightly before serving.

COOK'S TIP
If you cannot find pumpkin purée (available in cans), you can make your own at home. Peel, chop and deseed a small pumpkin or butternut squash. Chop the flesh into 5cm/2in pieces. Place the flesh in a large sheet of foil and sprinkle over 30ml/2 tbsp maple syrup and 15ml/1 tbsp ground cinnamon. Bake at 180°C/350°F/ Gas 4 for 30–40 minutes, or until the pumpkin is soft. Leave to cool slightly, then blitz to a purée in a blender. Store in the refrigerator until needed.

Nutritional information: Energy 195kcal/814kJ; Protein 3g; Carbohydrate 16g, of which sugars 3g; Fat 14g, of which saturates 5g; Cholesterol 3mg; Calcium 32mg; Fibre 0.9g; Sodium 125mg.

Snowmen pops

These tiny snowmen, made from light meringues with a chewy centre, decorated with orange noses and icing scarves, are almost too cute to eat. The meringues are quick and easy to prepare, and these keep well stored in an airtight container, so are ideal to make ahead of time.

5 Smooth the top of the second round using a clean finger. Bake for 1–1¼ hours, or until the meringues are dried and crisp. Leave them to cool completely on the baking sheets.

6 Sift the fondant icing sugar into a bowl and stir in enough water to give a smooth, thick icing. Divide the icing among three bowls and add black food colouring gel to one, orange to another and blue to the third.

MAKES 25

For the snowmen
2 egg whites
115g/4oz/generous ½ cup caster (superfine) sugar
100g/3¾oz/scant 1 cup fondant icing (confectioners') sugar
15–30ml/1–2 tbsp water
a few drops of black, orange and blue food colouring gels

To serve
25 thin wooden skewers

> **VARIATION**
> For 3D scarves, use thin red liquorice bootlaces, if you like.

1 Preheat the oven to 140°C/275°F/Gas 1. Line two baking sheets with silicone mats or baking parchment.

2 Place the egg whites in a bowl and whisk them until they hold stiff peaks. Gradually add the caster sugar, a tablespoonful at a time, whisking constantly until the meringue is shiny and glossy.

3 Using a piping (pastry) bag fitted with a large plain nozzle, pipe twenty-five 3cm/1¼in rounds on to the baking sheets.

4 Pipe a second, smaller round on top of each one to give a snowman shape, with a round body and smaller head.

7 Using three separate piping (pastry) bags, each fitted with a very small plain nozzle, pipe a small orange carrot nose, a thin blue scarf, three black buttons and two black eyes on to each snowman. Leave the icing to set, then insert a wooden skewer into the base of each snowman to serve.

Nutritional information: Energy 35kcal/148kJ; Protein 0g; Carbohydrate 9g, of which sugars 9g; Fat 0g, of which saturates 0g; Cholesterol 0mg; Calcium 1mg; Fibre 0g; Sodium 6mg.

Christmas tree pops

These dainty little trees, dusted with icing sugar snow and topped with a golden star, are perfect for Christmas celebrations. For best results, use long soft shredded coconut as this gives the best tree-like effect. Serve these festive little trees with a glass of mulled wine.

MAKES 28

For the cake
50g/2oz/¼ cup butter, softened
50g/2oz/¼ cup caster
  (superfine) sugar
1 egg
50g/2oz/½ cup self-raising
  (self-rising) flour
100g/3¾oz plain (semisweet)
  chocolate, melted
100g/3¾oz/scant ½ cup cream cheese
5ml/1 tsp ground cinnamon

For the decoration
150g/5oz/1⅔ cups long soft
  shredded coconut
a few drops of green food
  colouring gel
icing (confectioners') sugar,
  for dusting
25g/1oz ready-to-roll white
  icing (sugarpaste)
edible gold lustre spray
edible gold glitter
28 thin wooden skewers
250g/9oz white chocolate, melted

1 Preheat the oven to 180°C/350°F/ Gas 4. Grease and line a 20cm/8in square cake tin (pan).

2 For the cake, cream the butter and sugar together until light and fluffy. Beat in the egg. Sift in the flour and fold in. Spoon the cake mixture (batter) into the cake tin and level the surface.

3 Bake for 15–20 minutes, until golden and the tip of a sharp knife comes out clean when inserted into the centre. Turn out on to a wire rack to cool.

4 Process the cake to crumbs in a food processor. Transfer the cake crumbs to a bowl, add the melted plain chocolate, cream cheese and cinnamon and mix together.

5 Shape the mixture into 28 cones, 2cm/¾in in diameter and 3cm/1¼in in height. Place on a tray and chill in the freezer for 30 minutes. Meanwhile, for the decoration, mix the coconut with the green food colouring gel.

6 On an icing sugar-dusted surface, roll out the ready-to-roll icing to 5mm/ ¼in thickness. Cut out 28 stars using a tiny cutter. Place the stars on baking parchment, spray with gold lustre spray and sprinkle with gold glitter.

7 Press a skewer into the base of each cone. Dip each into the melted white chocolate, then roll in the green coconut. Add a star to the top of each tree, using melted white chocolate.

Nutritional information: Energy 114kcal/476kJ; Protein 1g; Carbohydrate 9g, of which sugars 8g; Fat 8g, of which saturates 5g; Cholesterol 15mg; Calcium 38mg; Fibre 0.7g; Sodium 42mg.

Gingerbread house pops

These little gingerbread houses look as if they have come straight from Hansel and Gretel's fairy story, embellished with white icing, chocolate buttons and a variety of sweets. The possibilities for decoration are endless – let your creative side run wild!

MAKES 16

For the biscuits (cookies)
120ml/8 tbsp black treacle (molasses)
120ml/8 tbsp golden
  (light corn) syrup
125g/4¼oz/8½ tbsp butter
300g/11oz/2¾ cups plain
  (all-purpose) flour, plus extra
  for dusting
10ml/2 tsp ground cinnamon
5ml/1 tsp ground ginger
5ml/1 tsp vanilla extract
5ml/1 tsp bicarbonate of soda
  (baking soda)
1 egg, beaten
16 ice lolly (popsicle) sticks

For the icing and decoration
360g/12½oz/generous 3 cups royal
  icing (confectioners') sugar
60ml/4 tbsp water
white chocolate buttons and sweets
  (candies), to decorate
edible glitter, for sprinkling

1 For the biscuits, put the black treacle, golden syrup and butter in a pan and heat gently until melted, stirring. Leave to cool slightly.

2 Sift the flour into a mixing bowl, add the cinnamon, ginger, vanilla extract and bicarbonate of soda, and mix.

3 Pour the cooled syrup into the flour mixture and stir together. Beat in the egg. The mixture will seem very soft. Leave the mixture to rest at room temperature for 1–2 hours, by which time it will be thick enough to roll.

4 Preheat the oven to 180°C/350°F/ Gas 4. Grease and line three baking sheets. On a flour-dusted surface, roll out the dough to 8mm/⅜in thickness. Cut out 16 gingerbread houses, by hand or with a large house-shaped cutter. Transfer to the baking sheets.

5 Insert a stick into the base of each biscuit, ensuring that the top of the stick is completely covered in dough. Bake for 10–12 minutes, until slightly risen. Leave the biscuits on the baking sheets for a few minutes, then transfer them to a wire rack to cool.

6 For the icing, sift the royal icing sugar into a bowl, add the water and whisk until the icing holds a peak when you lift the whisk up. Spoon the icing into a piping (pastry) bag fitted with a small plain nozzle.

7 You need to ice and decorate the biscuits one at a time, otherwise the icing will set and the sweets will not stick. Pipe some icing on to the roof area and along the base of the house. Pipe windows and a door, decorate with chocolate buttons and sweets, and sprinkle with edible glitter. Leave to set before serving.

Nutritional information: Energy 265kcal/1118kJ; Protein 3g; Carbohydrate 49g, of which sugars 34g; Fat 8g, of which saturates 5g; Cholesterol 32mg; Calcium 83mg; Fibre 0.7g; Sodium 164mg.

Christmas pudding pops

Every Christmas, we make our Christmas pudding following a recipe from my great-great-grandmother. My aunt started a new tradition when I was a child with a giant chocolate tiffin shaped like a Christmas pudding, decorated with glacé icing and topped with holly and berries. These pops are my version!

MAKES 30

For the cake
50g/2oz/¼ cup butter, softened
50g/2oz/¼ cup caster
  (superfine) sugar
1 egg
50g/2oz/½ cup self-raising
  (self-rising) flour, sifted
5ml/1 tsp ground Christmas
  cake spice
5ml/1 tsp ground cinnamon
100g/3¾oz white chocolate, melted
100g/3¾oz/scant ½ cup cream cheese
30 lollipop sticks

For the chocolate ganache
200g/7oz plain (semisweet)
  chocolate, chopped
30g/1¼oz/2½ tbsp butter
105ml/7 tbsp double (heavy) cream

For the decoration
65g/2½oz white chocolate, melted
30 mini sugar holly decorations

1 Preheat the oven to 180°C/350°F/ Gas 4. Grease and line a 20cm/8in square cake tin (pan).

2 For the cake, cream the butter and sugar until light and fluffy. Beat in the egg. Sift in the flour and fold in with the spices. Spoon the mixture (batter) into the cake tin and level the surface.

3 Bake for 15–20 minutes, until the cake springs back when pressed and the tip of a sharp knife comes out clean when inserted into the centre. Turn out on to a wire rack to cool.

4 Process the cooled cake to crumbs in a food processor. Transfer the crumbs to a mixing bowl, add the melted white chocolate and cream cheese, and mix together. Shape the mixture into 30 balls, 2cm/¾in in diameter. Place the balls on a tray and chill them in the freezer for 30 minutes.

5 Meanwhile, make the ganache. Place the plain chocolate, butter and double cream in a heatproof bowl set over a pan of simmering water, taking care that the water does not touch the bottom of the bowl. Stir until you have a smooth, glossy sauce. Remove the bowl from the heat and leave the ganache to cool and thicken.

6 Press a stick into each ball. Dip each ball into the chocolate ganache, coating all over. Press the wooden skewers into a foam block to secure each pop and leave to set.

7 To decorate, dip the top of each ball into the melted white chocolate, then top with a sugar holly decoration, and leave to set. Chill until ready to serve.

Nutritional information: Energy 79kcal/328kJ; Protein1g; Carbohydrate 7g, of which sugars 7g; Fat 6g, of which saturates 3g; Cholesterol 16mg; Calcium 22mg; Fibre 0g; Sodium 34mg.

Index